History of Chemical Science

Biographies of Chemists Volume II

Dr. T. R. Swaroop

Prof. K. S. Rangappa

NOTION PRESS

NOTION PRESS

India. Singapore. Malaysia.

ISBN xxx-x-xxxxx-xx-x

Dedicated to all chemists who have contributed to the development of science

Contents

Foreword xvii

Preface xix

Acknowledgments xxi

1. Acharya Prafulla Chandra Ray (1861 – 1944) 25

2. Herbert Henry Dow (1866 – 1930) 26

3. Moses Gomberg (1866 – 1947) 27

4. Alfred Werner (1866-1919) 28

5. Arthur Amos Noyes (1866 – 1936) 28

6. Nikolai Matveevich Kischner (1867 – 1935) 29

7. Vera Yevstafievna Popova (1867 – 1896) 30

8. Auguste Georges Darzens (1867 – 1954) 31

9. Marie Curie (1867-1934) 31

10. Søren Peter Lauritz Sørensen (1868 – 1939) 32

11. Fritz Haber (1868-1934) 33

12. Theodore William Richards (1868 – 1928) 34

13. Willis Rodney Whitney (1868 – 1958) 35

14. David Leonard Chapman (1869 – 1958) 35

15. Ernst Julius Cohen (1869 – 1944) 36

16. Fritz Pregl (1869 – 1930) 36

17. Richard Abegg (1869–1910) 37

18. Alekséy Y Chichibábin (1871-1945) 38

19. Max E A Bodenstein (1871 –1942) 38

20. Ernest Rutherford (1871-1937) 39

21. François A V Grignard (1871-1935) 40

22. Morris William Travers (1872 – 1961) ... 41

23. Georges Urbain (1872 – 1938) ... 41

24. Richard M Willstätter (1872 – 1942) ... 42

25. Nevil V Sidgwick (1873 – 1952) ... 43

26. Lev Aleksandrovich Chugaev (1873 – 1922) ... 44

27. Hans von Euler-Chelpin (1873 – 1964) ... 44

28. Martin Lowry (1874-1936) ... 45

29. Carl Bosch (1874 – 1940) ... 46

30. Chaim A Weizmann (1874 – 1952) ... 46

31. Gilbert N Lewis (1875-1946) ... 47

32. Karl Theophil Fries (1875 – 1962) ... 47

33. Heinrich Houben (1875 - 1940) ... 48

34. Erik C Clemmensen (1876 – 1941) ... 48

35. Adolf Windaus (1876 – 1959) ... 49

36. Alfred Stock (1876 – 1946) ... 49

37. Otto Diels (1876 – 1954) ... 50

38. Frederick Soddy (1877 –1956) ... 50

39. Francis W Aston (1877 – 1945) ... 51

40. Heinrich O Wieland (1877 – 1957) ... 52

41. Franz J Emil Fischer (1877–1947) ... 53

42. Julius Nieuwland (1878 – 1936) ... 53

43. Johannes N Brønsted (1879-1947) ... 54

44. Hans Meerwein (1879–1965) ... 54

45. Otto Hahn (1879 – 1968) ... 55

46. Henry Drysdale Dakin (1880 – 1952) ... 56

47. Claude Silbert Hudson (1881 – 1952) ... 56

48. Irving Langmuir (1881-1957) ... 57

49. Hans Fischer (1881 – 1945) 57

50. Hermann Staudinger (1881 –1965) 58

51. Walter N Haworth (1883-1950) 58

52. Peter J W Debye (1884 – 1966) 59

53. Friedrich K R Bergius (1884 – 1949)..................... 60

54. Theodor Svedberg (1884 – 1971).......................... 60

55. George A L Sarton (1884 – 1956) 61

56. Chika Kuroda (1884 – 1968) 61

57. Fritz Arndt (1885-1969), ... 62

58. Max Volmer (1885 – 1965)................................... 62

59. Satoyasu Iimori (1885 – 1982).............................. 63

60. George Hevesy (1885 – 1966)............................... 63

61. Robert Robinson (1886 – 1975) 64

62. Kazimierz Fajans (1887 –1975) 64

63. Akira Ogata (1887 - 1978) 65

64. James Batcheller Sumner (1887 – 1955)................ 65

65. Leopold Ružička (1887 – 1976)............................ 65

66. Paul Karrer (1889 – 1971) 66

67. Jaroslav Heyrovský (1890 – 1967)........................ 66

68. John H Northrop (1891 – 1987) 67

69. Alice Augusta Ball (1892 – 1916)......................... 67

70. Homer Burton Adkins (1892–1949)...................... 68

71. Johannes Martin Bijvoet (1892 – 1980) 68

72. James Bryant Conant (1893 – 1978) 69

73. Harold Clayton Urey (1893 – 1981) 70

74. Christopher K Ingold (1893 – 1970) 71

75. Henry Gilman (1893 – 1986) 71

CONTENTS

76. Leonora Bilger (1893 – 1975) 72

77. Francis Simon (1893 –1956) 72

78. Jnanendra Nath Mukherjee (1893 – 1983) 73

79. Jnan Chandra Ghosh (1894 –1959) 74

80. Izzal Kolthoff (1894-1993) 75

81. Shanti Swaroop Bhatnagar (1894 –1955) 75

82. Margaret Dorothy Foster (1895 – 1970) 76

83. Herman Francis Mark (1895 - 1992) 76

84. Morris Selig Kharasch (1895 – 1957) 77

85. Artturi I Virtanen (1895 – 1973) 77

86. William F Giauque (1895 – 1982) 78

87. Wallace H Carothers (1896 – 1937) 78

88. Leonid Andrussow (1896 –1988) 79

89. Robert S Mulliken (1896-1986) 79

90. Erich Hückel (1896 – 1980). 80

91. Nikolay N Semyonov (1896 – 1986) 80

92. Joseph H Simons (1897 – 1984) 81

93. Tadeusz Reichstein (1897 – 1996) 81

94. Cyril N Hinshelwood (1897 – 1967) 82

95. Ronald G W Norrish (1897 – 1978) 82

96. Irène Joliot-Curie (1897 – 1956) 83

97. Georg Wittig (1897 – 1987) 83

98. Karl W Ziegler (1898 – 1973) 84

99. Huang Minlon (1898 – 1979) 84

100. Katharine B Blodgett (1898 – 1979) 85

101. Robert Sidney Cahn (1899 – 1981) 85

102. Charles Prévost (1899-1983) 86

103. Paul Hermann Müller (1899 – 1965)..................... 86

104. John Butler (1899 – 1977).................................... 87

105. Jean F Joliot-Curie (1900 – 1958) 87

106. Richard Johann Kuhn (1900 – 1967)................... 88

107. Shirō Akabori (1900 – 1992) 88

108. Vincent du Vigneaud (1901 – 1978) 89

109. Werner Emmanuel Bachmann (1901 – 1951)...... 89

110. Linus Carl Pauling (1901 – 1994) 90

111. Henry Eyring (1901 – 1981)................................ 90

112. Kurt Alder (1902 – 1958).................................... 91

113. Arne Tiselius (1902 – 1971) 91

114. Lars Onsager (1903 – 1976)................................ 92

115. Giulio Natta (1903 – 1979)................................. 92

116. Adolf Butenandt (1903 – 1995) 93

117. Charles John Pedersen (1904 – 1989) 93

118. Wendell M Stanley (1904 – 1971) 94

119. Carolina Henriette MacGillavry (1904 – 1993) ... 94

120. Daulat Singh Kothari (1906 – 1993).................... 95

121. Vladimir Prelog (1906 – 1998)............................ 95

122. Max Tishler (1906 – 1989).................................. 96

123. Hazel Gladys Bishop (1906 – 1998) 96

124. Luis Federico Leloir (1906 – 1987)...................... 97

125. Alexander R Todd (1907 – 1997) 97

126. Edwin M McMillan (1907 – 1991) 98

127. Mary Elliott Hill (1907–1969) 98

128. Edward Teller (1908-2003).................................. 99

129. Willard F Libby (1908 – 1980) 99

130. Myrtle Claire Bachelder (1908 – 1997) 100

131. Melvin Spencer Newman (1908 – 1993)............ 100

132. Arthur C Cope (1909-1966) 101

133. Archer Martin (1910 – 2002) 101

134. Dorothy Hodgkin (1910 – 1994) 102

135. Paul John Flory (1910 – 1985) 102

136. Jacques Lucien Monod (1910 – 1976) 103

137. Melvin Ellis Calvin (1911 – 1997) 103

138. William Howard Stein (1911 – 1980) 104

139. Ewart Jones (1911 – 2002)................................. 104

140. Glenn Theodore Seaborg (1912 – 1999)............ 105

141. Herbert Charles Brown (1912 – 2004) 105

142. Stanford Moore (1913 – 1982) 106

143. Richard Synge (1914 – 1994)............................. 106

144. Max F Perutz (1914 – 2002)............................... 107

145. Arthur John Birch (1915 – 1995) 107

146. Jeanne Beadle Burbank (1915 – 2002)............... 108

147. Henry Taube (1915 – 2005) 108

148. Jan Boldingh (1915 – 2003) 109

149. Arthur Donald Walsh (1916 – 1977).................. 109

150. Christian B Anfinsen Jr. (1916 – 1995) 110

151. Ronald Sydney Nyholm (1917 – 1971).............. 110

152. William S Knowles (1917-2012) 111

153. Robert B Woodward (1917 – 1979)................... 111

154. John Cornforth Jr., (1917 – 2013)...................... 112

155. Ilya R Prigogine (1917 – 2003)......................... 112

156. Herbert A Hauptman (1917 – 2011) 113

157. John Bennett Fenn (1917 - 2010) 113

158. Ernst Otto Fischer (1918 – 2007) 114

159. Frederick Sanger (1918 – 2013) 114

160. Kenichi Fukui (1918 – 1998) 115

161. Jacob Akiba Marinsky (1918 – 2005) 115

162. Derek Barton (1918 – 1998)........................... 116

163. Jens Christian Skou (1918 – 2018) 116

164. Paul Delos Boyer (1918 – 2018) 117

165. Lawrence E Glendenin (1918 – 2008)................ 117

166. Ralph G Pearson (1919-2022)......................... 118

167. William N Lipscomb Jr. (1919 – 2011).............. 118

168. Donald James Cram (1919 – 2001) 119

169. Rosalind E Franklin (1920 – 1958) 119

170. Peter Dennis Mitchell (1920 – 1992) 120

171. George Porter (1920 – 2002) 120

172. Geoffrey Wilkinson (1921 – 1996) 121

173. Robert B Merrifield (1921 – 2006) 121

174. George S Hammond (1921 – 2005)................... ..122

175. Isabella Karle (1921 – 2017) 122

176. John B Goodenough (1922-2023) 123

177. Rudolph A Marcus (1923-) 123

178. Walter Kohn (1923 – 2016).............................. 124

179. Hugh Longuet-Higgins (1923 – 2004) 124

180. Ronald Gillespie (1924-2021).......................... 125

181. John Anthony Pople (1925 – 2004) 125

182. Luis Cárdenas (1925 – 2004) 126

183. Robert J P Williams (1926 – 2015).................... 126

CONTENTS

184. Paul Berg (1926-2023) 127

185. Aaron Klug (1926 – 2018) 127

186. Irwin Allan Rose (1926 – 2015) 128

187. Manfred Eigen (1927-2019)................................ 128

188. George Andrew Olah (1927 – 2017)................... 129

189. Frank S Rowland (1927 – 2012) 129

190. Alan G MacDiarmid (1927 – 2007) 130

191. Osamu Shimomura (1928 – 2018) 130

192. Elias James Corey (1928-) 131

193. John Charles Polanyi (1929-) 131

194. Paul C Lauterbur (1929 – 2007)......................... 132

195. John Kenneth Stille (1930 – 1989)..................... 132

196. Stanley Lloyd Miller (1930 – 2007)................... 133

197. Frank Albert Cotton (1930 – 2007).................... 133

198. Dewan Singh Bhakuni (1930-2021) 134

199. Akira Suzuki (1930-) 134

200. Yves Chauvin (1930 – 2015) 135

201. Martin Karplus (1930-) 135

202. Richard F Heck (1931 – 2015).......................... 136

203. Walter Gilbert (1932-) 136

204. Dudley R Herschbach (1932-) 137

205. Michael Smith (1932-2000) 137

206. Richard Robert Ernst (1933-2021) 138

207. Paul Jozef Crutzen (1933-2021) 138

208. Robert Floyd Curl Jr. (1933-2022) 139

209. C N R Rao (1934-) 139

210. Ei-ichi Negishi (1935-2021)................................ 140

211. Yuan Tseh Lee (1936-) 140

212. Alan Jay Heeger (1936-) 141

213. Hideki Shirakawa (1936-) 141

214. Gerhard Ertl (1936-) 142

215. Avram Hershko (1937-) 142

216. Roald Hoffmann (1937-) 143

217. Robert Huber (1937-) 143

218. Ryoji Noyori (1938-) 144

219. Kurt Wüthrich (1938-)..................................... 144

220. Tomas R Lindahl (1938-) 145

221. Barbara S Askins (1939-) 145

222. Jean-Marie Lehn (1939-) 146

223. Sidney Altman (1939-2022) 146

224. Harold W Kroto (1939 – 2016) 147

225. Ada E Yonath (1939-) 147

226. Thomas A Steitz (1940 – 2018) 148

227. Arieh Warshel (1940-) 148

228. Joachim Frank (1940-) 149

229. Karl Barry Sharpless (1941-) 149

230. George Pearson Smith (1941-)........................ ..150

231. John Ernest Walker (1941-) 150

232. Dan Shechtman (1941-) 151

233. Michael S Whittingham (1941-) 151

234. James F Stoddart (1942-) 152

235. Jacques Dubochet (1942-) 152

236. Robert Howard Grubbs (1942-2021)................... 153

237. Johann Deisenhofer (1943-) 153

238. Mario Molina (1943-2020)................................. 154

239. Richard E Smalley (1943 – 2005) 154

240. Robert J Lefkowitz (1943-) 155

241. Louis E Brus (1943-)....................................... 155

242. Jean-Pierre Sauvage (1944-) 156

243. Kary Banks Mullis (1944 – 2019) 156

244. Richard Royce Schrock (1945-) 157

245. Richard Henderson (1945-)............................ ..157

246. Alexei Ekimov (1945-) 158

247. Ahmed H Zewail (1946 – 2016) 158

248. Paul Lawrence Modrich (1946-) 159

249. Aziz Sancar (1946-) 159

250. Roger David Kornberg (1947-) 160

251. Thomas Robert Cech (1947-)........................ ..160

252. Aaron Ciechanover (1947-) 161

253. Martin Lee Chalfie (1947-) 161

254. Michael Levitt (1947-) 162

255. Akira Yoshino (1948-) 162

256. Hartmut Michel (1948-) 163

257. Peter Agre (1949-) 163

258. Bernard L Feringa (1951-) 164

259. Gregory Paul Winter (1951-) 164

260. Venkatraman Ramakrishnan (1952-) 165

261. William Esco Moerner (1953-) 165

262. Morten Peter Meldal (1954-) 166

263. Brian Kent Kobilka (1955-) 166

264. Roderick MacKinnon (1956-) 167

265. Frances Hamilton Arnold (1956-) 167

266. Koichi Tanaka (1959-) 168

267. Robert Eric Betzig (1960-) 168

268. Moungi Bawendi (1961-) 169

269. Paul Anastas (1962-) 169

270. Stefan Walter Hell (1962-) 170

271. Jennifer Anne Doudna (1964-) 170

272. Carolyn R Bertozzi (1966-) 171

273. Emmanuelle Charpentier (1968-) 171

274. Benjamin List (1968-) 172

275. David W C MacMillan (1968-) 172

Foreword

The present publication is the second volume in the series of short biographies of chemists. It contains a short and lucid biography of 275 chemists as compared to 250 biographies contained in the first volume of this series. It opens with the biography of Late Acharya Prafulla Chandra Ray and ends with David W. C. McMillan encompassing 19th and 20th century chemists. The most remarkable fact about this book is that almost all chemists mentioned in this book are Nobel laureates. We seldom find books on history of science in general and chemical science in particular. As for as my knowledge goes, there are very few books such as Science in History in four volumes by J. D. Bernal and Science in India by B. V Subbarayappa, which throw light on the development of science. In this book, Prof. K. S. Rangappa and Dr. T. R. Swaroop have brought out in a lucid fashion the various facets of the developments in chemical science and technology in an exceedingly comprehensive manner. They have brought to bear their extraordinary scholarship in delving into the details of contributions of various scientists to chemistry, physics, biology and various aspects of medical science. A striking and unique aspect of their presentation relates to the coherent structuring of the evolution of ideas and knowledge in 19th and 20th centuries which demands the highest level of versatility and familiarity with the fundamental and applied sciences. In this book the authors have broadly outlined the development in science during the last two centuries in the world going through a chronological sequence of developments and covering the works of various chemistry Nobel laureates.

This book will be of immense value to students and teachers who have probably for the first time a book that can be used as a handbook to know the Chemists who have contributed immensely towards science. The book can act as catalyst for the students to tread the path as taken by these Nobel laureates who have left no stone unturned to make very useful Scientific discoveries. Students will definitely be inspired to develop the spirit of enquiry and scientific temper as enshrined in the Fundamental duties part in our Indian constitution.

I am glad to see that this book may become so popular and I hope it will serve the purpose for which it is intended.

Dr. K. N. Thimmaiah

Professor of Chemistry (Rtd)

Natural Science Department

Northwest Mississippi Community College

Desoto Center, Southaven, USA

Date: 1 May, 2024

.

Preface

Chemistry has developed due to breakthrough research by many chemists. Our intention is to collect shrot biographies of chemists and their contributions towards the development of chemistry. In our previous book on 'History of Chemical Science, Biographies of Chemists Volume I', we have presented the short biographies of chemists who were born between 300 AD and 1865. In continuation of this, we herein present a book on 'History of Chemical Science, Biographies of Chemists Volume II', which presents the biographies of chemists born from 1861 to 1968. We hope this book may inspire young generation to contribute more for the development of science.

We began collecting names of chemists whom we study in our undergraduate and graduate courses. Due to increasing number of chemists after 19th century, we restricted to collect biographies of only Nobel laureates. We have presented biographies of 275 chemists in this volume including Nobel laureates up to 2023.

Chemistry has developed more in the last century. During 18th century, Europeans lead the chemical science, in particular Germans. In 19th century, especially after World War II, Americans have contributed more, which is reflected by the fact that the highest number of Nobel laureates are from the United States of America.

Through our books, we insist Indian academicians and students to read history of chemical science in their spare time, which will inspire them to do more chemistry.

Dr. T. R. Swaroop (swarooptr@gmail.com)

Prof. K. S. Rangappa (rangappaks@yahoo.com)

Date: 8 May, 2024

Acknowledgments

Authors thank teaching faculty and non-teaching colleagues, administrative workers and researchers of the Department of Studies in Organic Chemistry, Institution of Excellence and Department of Studies in Chemistry, University of Mysore, Mysuru, Karnataka.

Authors are greatful to family members and friends for inspiring support during the journey of making this book.

Authors are greatful to Prof. N. K. Lokanath, Hon'ble Vice-Chancellor, University of Mysore, Mysuru, Karnataka and Dr. Basappa, Registrar (Evaluation), University of Mysore, Mysuru, Karnataka for memorable encouragement and support amidst their administrative works. We greatly extend our heartful thanks to Prof. K. Mantelingu and Mr. Mahesha K for reviewing this book.

We acknowledge Wikipedia for providing informations and images of chemists.

We thank Prof. K. N. Thimmaiah for writing foreword to this book.

We thank Notion Press for rapid publication of this book.

1. Acharya Prafulla Chandra Ray (1861 – 1944)

Sir Acharya Prafulla Chandra Ray was an Indian chemist, educationist, historian, industrialist and philanthropist born at Raruli-Katipara to Harish Chandra Raychowdhury and Bhubanmohini Devi. He is well known for the establishment of modern research school in chemistry. He is considered as the father of chemical science in India. He was the founder of Bengal Chemicals and Pharmeceuticals. He wrote a text book *"A History of Hindu Chemistry from the Earliest Times to the Middle of Sixteenths Century"*.

He got primary education at a village school run by his father. Later, he attended physics and chemistry lectures as an external student at the Presidency College. He was inspired by Alexander Pedler. In 1881, he passed FA exam in 1881 from the University of Calcutta. He won a scholarship to study B.Sc. at the University of Edinburgh. He sailed to United Kingdom in 1882 at the age of 21.

At Edinburgh, he began his studies under Alexander Crum Brown. Besides, he also studied under Robert Bunsen at the University of Heidelberg. In his doctoral study under Crum Brown, who was an organic chemist, Ray was also interested in inorganic chemistry.

In 1895, he started his work on nitrite chemistry. In 1896, he published a paper on preparation of mercurous nitrite. Another notable contribution of Ray was preparation of ammonium nitrite. He established a new Indian School of Chemistry in 1924. He was the president of the Indian Science Congress in 1920.

He retired from the Presidency College in 1916 and joined the Calcutta University College of Science, where he worked on platinum, gold, iridium etc.

He died in 1944 at Calcutta.

2. Herbert Henry Dow (1866 – 1930)

Herbert Henry Dow was a Canadian-born American chemical industrialist born in 1866 at Belleville to Americans Joseph Henry Dow and Sarah Bunnell. He is well known for the establishment of multinational conglomerate Dow Chemical. He was an inventor of chemical processes and was a successful businessman.

He was graduated from a high school in 1884. Later, he enrolled in the Case School of Applied Science. He conducted research on chemical composition of brines in Ohio. He discovered that brine samples from Canton, Ohio and Midland were very rich in bromine. He was graduated in 1888. He worked as a professor of chemistry at Huron Street Hospital College in Cleveland and continued research on extraction of chemicals from brine.

In 1889, he developed a method for the extraction of bromine. He patented this work later. He established his own company within a year. His associates were impressed with his work and encouraged him to establish the Midland Chemical Company in Midland, Michigan. He continued his work on extraction of bromine. In 1891, he developed the Dow process, which is a method for the extraction of bromine by electrolytic oxidation of bromide to bromine.

He wanted to expand his research on electrolysis to yield other chemicals. His financial backers did not approve his continued research and fired him from the Midland Chemical Company. Inspite of this, he developed methods for the extraction of chlorine and caustic soda from sodium chloride. His Dow Chemical Company focused on extraction of many more chemicals from brine.

World War I created a demand for goods from his company. He supplied wartime goods like magnesium, monochlorobenzene and phenol for explosives. He died in 1930 at Rochester.

3. Moses Gomberg (1866 – 1947)

Moses Gomberg was a Russian-born American chemist born in 1866 at Yelizavetgrad to Hershko Gomberg and Maryam-Ethel Reznikova.

In 1884, his family migrated to Chicago, where he worked at the Stock Yards while attending high school. He admitted to the University of Michigan in 1886 and received B.Sc. in 1890. In 1894, he received doctoral degree under the supervision of A. B. Prescott. He worked as a postdoctoral fellow with Baeyer and Thiele in Munich and with Victor Meyer in Heidelberg.

He worked at the University of Michigan and became chair of department of chemistry from 1927 to 1936. He served as president of the American Chemical Society in 1931.

During his attempts to synthesize sterically congested hydrocarbon hexaphenylethane, he discovered triphenyl radical. Hence he is considered as the founder of radical chemistry. This work was later followed up by Wilhelm Schlenk. Werner Emmanuel Bachmann was a student of Gomberg, with whom Gomberg discovered Gomberg-Bachmann reaction.

He died in 1947 at Ann Arbor.

The University of Michigan started new fellowships in his honor. In 2000, the centennial of his paper 'Triphenylmethyl, a Case of Trivalent Carbon', a symposium was held in his memory.

In 1993, the chemistry department of the University of Michigan instituted Moses Gomberg lecture series, which invites distinguished scientists to the chemistry department.

4. Alfred Werner (1866-1919)

Alfred Werner was a Swiss chemist born in 1866 at Mulhouse to Jean-Adam Werner and Salomé Jeanette Werner. He was a professor at the University of Zurich. He was awarded the Nobel Prize in Chemistry in 1913 for his idea of octahedral configuration of transition metal complexes. He was instrumental in developing the basics of coordination chemistry. He was the first inorganic chemist to win the Nobel Prize.

He received the Ph.D degree in 1890 from the University of Zürich. He was trained as a postdoctoral fellow at Paris. Later, he returned to the Swiss Federal Institute in 1890. He moved to University of Zurich as a professor. In 1894, he became a Swiss citizen.

In 1893, he was the first to propose structures of coordination compounds, in which a central transition metal atom is surrounded by neutral or anionic ligands.

He suffered from arteriosclerosis in brain. He died in a psychiatric hospital in Zurich in 1919.

5. Arthur Amos Noyes (1866 – 1936)

Arthur Amos Noyes was a U.S. chemist, inventor and educator born in 1866 at Newburyport. He received his doctoral degree in 1890 from Leipzig University under the supervision of Wilhelm Ostwald.

He was a professor at California Institute of Technology from 1919 to 1936. He influenced educational philosophy and creation of National Research Council. He served as trustee for Society for Science and the Publics.

He died in 1936 at Californic at the age of 69.

6. Nikolai Matveevich Kischner (1867 – 1935)

Nikolai Matveyevich Kischner was a Russian chemist and member of Russian Academy of Sciences born in 1867 in Moscow.

He was graduated from the Moscow Classical Gymnasium. In 1886, he enrolled at the Moscow State University as Faculty of Physics and Mathematics.

After 1889, he focussed on organic chemistry and studied under Vladimir Luginin and Vladimir Markovnikov. He received doctoral degree on 'Amines and hydrazines of polymethylene series, methods of their preparation and transformation' in 1895. In 1900, he defended a habilitation on 'The action of silver oxide and hydroxylamine on bromamines: On the structure of hexahydrobenzene'. During his work with Markovnikov, he assisted him with teaching. Later, he taught courses in organic chemistry at the Moscow University and the Alexander Military School.

In 1901, he was appointed as professor of organic chemistry of the Tomsk Polytechnique University. He left this job in 1913 and returned to Moscow. In Moscow, he continued to work until his death.

In the beginning, he studied the hydrogenation of benzene using hydroiodic acid. Between 1907 and 1910, he worked on synthesis of cyclobutane ester and studied transformation of cyclobutane into cyclopentane. In 1911, he extended this work on cyclopropane. In 1910, he described the catalytic decomposion of alcylidehydrazines, which was later called as Wolff-Kishner reduction.

In 1912, he applied the catalytic decomposition to pyrazoline bases and developed a method for the preparation of substituted cyclopropanes by the thermal decomposition pyrazolines.

He died in 1935 at Moscow.

7. Vera Yevstafievna Popova (1867 – 1896)

Vera Yevstafievna Popova was a Russian chemist born in 1867 at Saint Petersburg to Evstafy Ivanovich Bogdanovsky. She was married to General Jacob Kozmich Popov in 1895. She was one of the first chemists in Russia. She was the first female, who wrote a chemistry textbook in Russia.

She started early education at the age of 11 at the Smolny Institute. She studied Bestuzhev courses for four years. Later, she worked for two years at the Academy of Sciences and the Military Surgical Academy.

In 1889, she moved to Switzerland, where she worked for her doctoral degree at the University of Geneva on dibenzyl ketone. She also worked with Dr. Philippe Auguste in Geneva, who was working on stereochemistry.

She returned to Saint Petersburg in 1892 and worked at the Bestuzhev Courses by teaching. Later, she worked as an assistant to Prof. L'vov. She wrote a textbook on basic chemistry. She wrote many reviews and translated many papers on chemistry. From 1891 to 1894, she published many papers based on her doctoral thesis.

She was not only a chemist, but also an entomologist.

Her husband was a director of a military steel plant and hence she demanded a laboratory, where she can continue her chemistry. She was given a tribute in the Journal of the Russian Physical Chemical Society.

She died in 1896 at the age of 28 in an accidental explosion, which occurred during the synthesis of methylidynephosphane (H-C≡P), which is similar to hydrogen cyanide. Her early death led his husband to raise a fund in her memory for female students.

8. Auguste Georges Darzens (1867 – 1954)

Auguste Georges Darzens was a Russian-born French chemist born in 1867. He studied at École Polytechnique in Paris under Louis Édouard Grimaux. In 1899, he received dotoral degree in medicine. Between 1913 and 1937, he was a professor of chemistry at the École Polytechnique. In parallel, he served as a director of a research laboratory at LT Piver, a perfumery outfit. 

In 1904, he discovered Darzens reaction. His other contributions were Darzens tetralin synthesis, Darzens halogenation and the Darzens synthesis of unsaturated ketones. He has written a textbook on '*Initiation chimique*', which was translated into English in 1913 under the title 'Chemistrty'.

He died in 1954.

9. Marie Curie (1867-1934)

Marie Salomea Skłodowska Curie was a Poland-born French chemist born in 1867 at Warsaw. She married French physicist Pierre Curie. She worked on radioactivity. She was the first woman to win a Nobel Prize and the first person and the only women, to win the Nobel Prize twice. She was a professor at the University of Paris. She  won Nobel Prize in chemistry in 1911. She discovered elements polonium and radium. She studied at the Flying University. In 1891, she moved to France. She founded Curie Institute in Paris in 1920 and at Warsaw in 1932. During World War I, she developed mobile radiography units to help hospitals and provide X-ray services.

She died in 1934 at the age of 66.

10. Søren Peter Lauritz Sørensen (1868 – 1939)

Søren Peter Lauritz Sørensen was a Danish chemist born in 1868 at Havrebjerg.

He is well known for the introduction of the concept of pH, which is a scale to measure acidity and alkalinity.

He studied at University of Copenhagen. He wanted to study medicine but switched over to study chemistry by the influence of chemist S. M. Jørgensen.

During his doctoral study, he worked as assistant in chemistry at the Danish Polytechnic Institute. Also, he worked as a consultant for the Royal Naval Dockyard.

Between 1901 and 1938, he was head of the Carlsberg Laboratory, Copenhagen, where he studied the effect of ions on protein concentration.

He died in 1939 at Copenhagen.

11. Fritz Haber (1868-1934)

Fritz Haber was a German-Jewish chemist born in 1868 at Breslau to Siegfried and Paula Haber. He was awarded the Nobel Prize in Chemistry in 1918 for the manufacture of ammonia from nitrogen and hydrogen gases, which was popularly known as Haber-Bosch process. This invention is responsible for the large scale production of fertilizers and  explosives. He with Max-Born, proposed a new method for the evaluation of lattice energy of an ionic solid. He is considered as the father of chemical warfare for his pioneering work on development of chlorine and other poisonous gases during World War I.

He was primarily educated at the Johanneum School and the St. Elizabeth classical school. Later, he studied chemistry at the Friedrich Wilhelm University in Berlin. He also studied at Heidelberg University under Robert Bunsen. He served in Army for sometime and returned to Charlottenburg, where he became a student of Carl Liebermann. In addition to his lectures, he also attended lectures by Otto Witt on chemical technology of dyes.

At first, he worked as assistant to Ludwig Knorr at the University of Jena, Carl Engler at the University of Karlsruhe and with Hans Bunte. He worked on decomposition of hydrocarbons with Bunte. He worked on electrochemistry as well. He became associate professor. In 1906, he was appointed as professor.

He served as captain in World War I. He developed chlorine and other deadly gases in war. He also developed gas masks with adsorbent, which can filter such gases. He was in competition with French Nobel laureate Victor Grignard for the development of chemical warfares.

He once said, 'during peace time a scientist belongs to the World, but during war time he belongs to his country'.

He died in 1934 at Bassel.

12. Theodore William Richards (1868 – 1928)

Theodore William Richards was an American chemist born in 1868 at Germantown to William Trost Richards and Anna nee Matlack. He was married to Miriam Stuart Thayer in 1896. He won the Nobel Prize in Chemistry for determination of atomic weights of chemical elements.

He worked with Prof. Josiah Parsons Cooke of Harvard. Later, his family spent two years in Europe, where he worked more on science. After his retuen to United States, he studied at Haveford College. He then enrolled at the Harvard University and received B.A degree in 1886. He continued work at Harvard on determination of atomic weight of oxygen relative to hydrogen under the supervision of Josiah Parsons Cooke. In the next year, he studied under Victor Meyer at the University of Göttingen as a postdoctoral fellow.

He returned to Harvard as an assistant in chemistry, then instructor and assistant professor and finally professor in 1901. In 1903, he became chairman of the chemistry department. In 1912, he became Erving Professor of Chemistry and Director of the new Wolcott Gibbs Memorial Laboratory.

Majority of his research was focussed on determination of atomic weights. He determined atomic weights of nearly 55 elements with his students. He showed the existence of different atomic weights, by observing the atomic weights of lead from natural origin and radioactive decay.

His other works include compressibilities of atoms, heats of solution and neutralization, and the elctrochemistry of amalgams. His investigation on determination of electrochemical potentials at low temperature led to the Nernst heat theorem and Third law of thermodynamics. He invented the adiabatic calorimeter and the nephelometer, which were used for the determination of atomic weight of strontium.

He died in 1928 at Cambridge.

13. Willis Rodney Whitney (1868 – 1958)

Willis Rodney Whitney was an Americaan chemist born in 1868 at Jamestown. He was the founder of General Electric Company. He received B.Sc. degree from the Massachusetts Institute of Technology and worked there as an assistant instructor of chemistry until 1892. He studied for Ph.D degree at the University of Leipzig under Wilhelm Ostwald. He worked on electrochemistry and developed electrochemical theory of corrosion.

He worked as an advisor to the newly founded research lab of General Electric Company and joined this company with full job. He with Irving Langmuir and William David Coolidge worked on vacuum and gas-filled lamps, telegraph and X-ray technology.

He died in 1958 at Schenectady.

14. David Leonard Chapman (1869 – 1958)

David Leonard Chapman was an Engish chemist born in 1869 at Wells, Norfolk. He is associated with Chapman –Jouguet treatment and Gouy-Chapman model.

He was a fellow of Jesus College, Oxford for 37 years. He attended Manchester Grammer School for primary education. Later he went to Christ Church, Oxford to get degrees in chemistry and physics. He worked at the University of Manchester. He was apponiteed as fellow and tutor at Jesus College. He became the vice-principal of this college.

Photochemical reaction between hydrogen and chlorine caught his attention. He postulated steady state hypothsis in 1923.

He died in 1958 because of cancer.

15. Ernst Julius Cohen (1869 – 1944)

Ernst Julius Cohen was a Dutch Jewish chemist born in 1869 at Amsterdam. He is popular for his work on allotropy of metals. He studied chemistry under Svante Arrheious at Stockholm and Henri Moissan at Paris and van't Hoff at Amsterdam.

In 1893, he became assistant to van't Hoff. In 1902, he became professor of chemistry at the Universityof Utrecht.

He became member of the Royal Netherlands Academy of Arts and Sciences in 1913. He was elected to the Royal Society as a member in 1926.

He was killed in 1944 in a gas chamber at Auschwitz concentration camp.

16. Fritz Pregl (1869 – 1930)

Fritz Pregl was a Slovenian and Austrian chemist and physician born in 1869. He received the Nobel Prize in Chemistry for his contributions on qualitative organic microanalysis and combustion train technique for elemental analysis.

He started his career as chemist and then studied medicine at the University of Graz. He observed limitations in quantitative organic microanalysis. This inspired him to develop process of elemental analysis.

He died in 1930 at Graz.

In 1950, the department of the University of Graz, where Fritz worked, became Institute of Medical Chemistry and Pregl Laboratory.

17. Richard Abegg (1869–1910)

Richard Wilhelm Heinrich Abegg was a German chemist born in 1869 at Danzig to Wilhelm Abegg and Margarete Friedenthal. He is well known for the development of valence theory. He stated that the difference of the maximum positive and negative valence of an element tends to be eight. This rule has become popular as Abegg's rule.

He studied at the University of Kiel and the University of Tübingen. He got his doctoral degree from the University of Berlin under the guidance of August Wilhelm von Hofmann. After obtaining his Ph.D degree, he began research on physical chemistry while studying under Friedrich Wilhelm Ostwald in Leipzig. Later, he worked as assistant to Walther Nernst at the University of Göttingen and to Svante Arrhenius at the University of Stockholm.

He proposed the theory of freezing-point depression. Besides, he worked on dielectric constants, osmotic pressure, oxidation potentials and complex ions.

He became professor of chemistry at the University of Breslau. After two years, he became a Privatdozent at the Wroclaw University of Technology, Poland. With his colleague Guido Bodländer, he published on electroaffinity.

He served as editor of *Zeitschrift für Elektrochemie* from 1901 until his death.

He died in 1910 at Köslin.

18. Alekséy Y Chichibábin (1871-1945)

Alekséy Yevgényevich Chichibábin was a Russian chemist born in 1871 at Kuzemin. He was married to Vera Vladimirovna.

He studied at the University of Moscow and received his doctoral degree from the University of St. Petersburgh. He became professor of chemistry at the Imperial College of Technology in Moscow in 1909. Later, he moved to Paris. He started work at Collège de France and remained there until his death. He served as director at French dye and fine chemical manufacturer, and advisor to Schering and Roosevelt Co. of New York.

He contributed for several organic chemical reactions. He developed a novel route for the synthesis of terpyridine, which became popular as Chichibabin pyridine synthesis. The other reactions include Bodroux-Chichibabin aldehyde synthesis and the Chichibabin reaction.

He died in 1945 at Paris.

19. Max E A Bodenstein (1871 –1942)

Max Ernst August Bodenstein was a German chemist born in 1871 at Magdeburg to Magdeburg merchant and brewer Franz Bodenstein. He was married to Elise Meissner. He is popular for his work on chemical kinetics and he is considered as one of the founders of it.

He was the first to postulate a chain reaction mechanism, where explosions are possible.

He studied at the University of Heidelberg for doctoral degree under Victor Meyer. He studied with Karl Liebermann at the Technical University of Berlin-Charlottenburg and with Walther Nernst at the University of Göttingen. In 1936, he was awarded the August Wilhelm von Hofmann votive medal. He died in 1942 at Berlin.

20. Ernest Rutherford (1871-1937)

Ernest Rutherford was a New Zealand scientist born in 1871 at Brightwater to James Rutherford and Martha Thompson. He discovered the concept of radioactive half-life. He discovered the nuclear radiations as alpha and beta. He won the Nobel Prize in Chemistry for his work on disintegration of elements and chemistry of radioactive substances.

He with Thomas Royds discovered that alpha particle is actually helium nuclei in his gold foil experiment. He conducted the first artificially induced nuclear radiation in 1917, where nitrogen nuclei were bombarded with alpha particles.

He became the Director of the Cavendish Laboratory at the University of Cambridge in 1919. Under his captaincy, the neutron was discovered by James Chadwick in 1932. In the same year, his students John Cockcroft and Ernest Walton conducted an experiment to split the nucleus in a controlled manner.

In 1898, he moved to McGill University, Canada. In 1901, he received D.Sc. from the University of New Zealand. In 1907, he returned to the Victoria University of Manchester. He was knighted in 1914.

During World War I, he worked on problems of submarine detection by sonar. In 1916, he was awarded the Hector Memorial Medal. He forced the New Zealand government to support education and research, which led to the establishment of Department of Scientific and Industrial Research (DSIR). He served as the president of the Royal Society between 1925 and 1930. In 1933, he received T. K. Sidey Medal from the Royal Society of New Zealand.

He died in 1937 at Cambridge. He was buried in Westminster Abbey beside Sir Isaac Newton. The chemical element rutherfordium (element 104) was named after him in 1997.

21. François A V Grignard (1871-1935)

François Auguste Victor Grignard was a French chemist born in 1871 at Cherbourg.

He served in army for a year. Later, he returned to the University of Lyon to study mathematics. He next studied chemistry under Philippe Barbier and Louis Bouveault.

He worked on stereochemistry and enines, with which he was not satisfied. He asked Barbier for a new problem. Barbier advised him about the success of Saytzeff reaction after using magnesium instead of zinc. They synthesized alcohols from alkyl halides, aldehydes, ketones and alkenes. Grignard hypothesized that aldehyde/ketone prevented reaction of magnesium with alkyl haide, which resulted in low yields. He started reaction by adding magnesium to alkyl halide in anhydrous ether followed by the addition of aldehyde/ketone, which drastically increased the yield of reaction. After few years, he was able to isolate the intermediate, which became popular as the Grignard reagent.

He joined the University of Nancy as professor in 1910. He and Paul Sabatier were awarded the Nobel Prize in Chemistry in 1912. During World War I, he worked on chemical warfares, particularly on the manufacture of phosgene and detection of mustard gas. In 1918, he discovered that sodium iodide can be used as a battlefield test for mustard gas. His counterpart on the German side was another Nobel Prize-winner Fritz Haber.

He died in 1935 at Lyon.

22. Morris William Travers (1872 – 1961)

Morris William Travers was an English chemist born in 1872 at Kensington. He worked with Sir William Ramsay for the discovery of xenon, neon and krypton. He was the founder director of Indian Institute of Science in India.

He heated minerals and meteorites in the search for further gases, but found none. In 1898, they subjected a large quantity of liquid air to fractional distillation and discovered krypton from it. They examined the argon fraction to get a lower boiling point constituent, which was neon. In a similar way, they discovered krypton.

In 1904, he became professor of chemistry at University College. In 1904, he was selected as a Fellow of the Royal Society.

He died in 1961 at Stroud.

23. Georges Urbain (1872 – 1938)

Georges Urbain was a French chemist born in 1872 at Paris. He focussed his work on rare earths. He discovered the element lutetium. He conducted research on efflorescence of saline hydrates.

He served as member of the Institut de France and director of the Institute of Chemistry in Paris. During World War I, he served in the Ministry of War as a laboratory director and technical advisor for artillery and explosives. He was also appointed as head of the chemistry section of the Palais de la Découverte, director of the Chemical Treatment laboratory of Thiais and the president of Ecole Pratique des Hautes Etudes.

He died in 1938 at Paris.

24. Richard M Willstätter (1872 – 1942)

Richard Martin Willstätter was a German chemist born in 1872 at Karlsruhe to Maxwell Willstätter and Sophie Ulmann. He worked on structure of plant pigments and chlorophyll. He won the Nobel Prize in Chemistry in 1915 for this study.

He got primary education at Karlsruhe Gymnasium. He entered University of Munich to study science at the age of 18. He studied under Alfred Einhorn and received his doctoral degree on structure of cocaine in 1894. He continued research on alkaloids and synthesized several of them. In 1902, he became professor.

He left Munich and became professor at the ETH Zürich in 1905, where he worked on chlorophyll. He first suggested its empirical formula.

In 1912, he was appointed as professor of chemistry at the University of Berlin and director of the Kaiser Wilhelm Institute for Chemistry, where he worked on determination of structure of pigments of flowers and fruits. Here he disclosed the fact that chlorophyll is composed of two compounds - chlorophyll a and chlorophyll b.

In 1915, Fritz Haber asked him to work on poisonous gases during World War I. He did not accept the invitation but instead worked on protection. He and his co-workers developed a three layer filter, which absorbed all of the enemy's gases. Thirty million were manufactured in 1917. He was awarded the Iron Cross Second Class.

In 1916, he returned to Munich. During 1920s, he worked on investigation of enzyme reactions and disclosed a fact that enzymes are chemical substances not biological organisms.

In 1939, he emigrated to Switzerland.

He died of a heart attack in 1842 at Muralto.

25. Nevil V Sidgwick (1873 – 1952)

Nevil Vincent Sidgwick was an English chemist born in 1873 at Oxford to William Carr Sidgwick and Sarah Isabella. He was unmarried. His notable works are development of theory of valency and chemical bonding.

He was educated at Summer Fields School and Rugby School. He spent some time with Wilhelm Ostwald in Germany. Because of illness he returned home. In 1899, he joined University of Tübingen to work under Hans von Pechmann. He received D.Sc. for his work on acetone-dicarboxylic acid. He was elected to a fellowship at Lincoln College where he spent rest of his time.

In 1914, he was one of the members of the party, which was choosen to represent the British Association for the meeting held in Australia. He understood the atomic structure and explained chemical bonding in complexes. He demonstrated the existence of hydrogen bonding.

He was elected to the Royal Society as a member in 1822.

In 1927, he proposed inert pair effect in p-block atoms. He correlated the molecular geometry with number of the valence electrons on a central atom. These ideas were later developed into the VSEPR theory.

The scope and significance of his researches brought him international fame.

He travelled to Toronto for a British Association meeting in 1924 and explored much in Canada. He spent some time in Cornell University and Princeton University.

He returned to Oxford and worked on some textbooks. He travelled a lot in United States after 1930s.

He died in 1952 at Oxford.

26. Lev Aleksandrovich Chugaev (1873 – 1922)

Lev Aleksandrovich Chugaev was a Russian chemist born in 1873 at Moscow. He was a professor at the University of Petersburg. He was active in organic chemistry and inorganic chemistry.

He discovered the formation of complex when dimethylglyoxime is treated with nickel(II) ions. He contributed more to platinum chemistry. Chloropentammineplatinum(IV) ion is called as "Chugaev's salt". He also studied complexes of hydrazine. He discovered Chugaev reaction during his work on thujene and terpene.

He died in 1922 at Gryazovets.

27. Hans von Euler-Chelpin (1873 – 1964)

Hans Karl August Simon von Euler-Chelpin was a German born Swedish chemist born in 1873 at Augsburg. He was married to Astrid Cleve. He won the Nobel Prize in Chemistry in 1929 for his work on fermentation of sugar by enzymes. He was a professor at Stockholm University. His son Ulf von Euler won the Nobel Prize in Physiology or Medicine in 1970.

He studied chemistry under Emil Fischer at the University of Berlin. In 1895, he received his doctoral degree. He was appointed to teach Privatdozent in the Royal University at Stockholm, where he visited the laboratoty of van't Hoff. Many people influenced him to study along with Nernst.

In 1902, he took Swedish citizenship. In 1906, he was appointed as a professor at the Royal University at Stockholm.

He died in 1964 at Stockholm.

28. Martin Lowry (1874-1936)

Thomas Martin Lowry was an English chemist born in 1874 at Low Moor to Reverend E. P. Lowry. He is well known for the development of Brønsted-Lowry acid–base theory.

He was educated at Kingswood School and Central Technical College. He was interested in the study of chemistry. He studied chemistry under Henry Edward Armstrong, whose interests were on organic chemistry and nature of ions in aqueous solutions.

Between 1904 and 1913, he worked as lecturer at the Westminster Training College. In 1913, he became the head of the chemical development in Guy's Hospital and professor at the University of London. From 1920, he served as Chair of Physical Chemistry at the University of Cambridge.

He was a member and president to the Faraday Society. He was elected to the Royal Society in 1914. He was the ditector of shell-filling and worked for the Trench Warfare Committee, Chemical Warfare Committee and Ordnance Committee during World War I. For this service, he got the Order of the British Empire and the Order of Saints Maurice and Lazarus.

In 1898, he observed the change in optical rotation on nitrocamphor with time. He called this phenomenon as muta rotation. He studied changes in optical rotations of camphor derivatives catalyzed by acid and base.

He published many papers and several books.

He died in 1936 at Cambridge.

29. Carl Bosch (1874 – 1940)

Carl Bosch was a German chemist born in 1874 at Cologne to Carl Friedrich Alexander Bosch. He won the Nobel Prize in Chemistry. He was a piooner in the area of high pressure industrial chemistry.

He studied at the Technische Hochsschule Charlottenburg and the University of Leipzig. He received Ph.D degree in 1898 in organic chemistry. Later, he worked at BASF.

He died in 1940 at Heidelberg.

30. Chaim A Weizmann (1874 – 1952)

Chaim Azriel Weizmann was a Russian born Israeli chemist born in 1874. He was elected as the first president of Israel. He is considered as the father of industrial fermentation. He developed acetone-butanol-ethanol fermentation process. His acetone production method was of great inportance in the manufacture of explosive cordite. This was used extensively by British army in World War I.

He was the founder of Sieff Research Institute in Israel, which later became Weizmann Institute of Science. He was instrumental in the establishment of Hebrew University of Jerusalem.

In 1899, he received his doctoral degree in organic chemistry. Later, he joined University of Geneva. In 1901, he was appointed as assistant lecturer at the University of Geneva. In 1904, he moved to the University of Manchester as a senior lecturer. He got British citizenship in 1910. Later, he became the first president of Israel.

He died in 1952 at Rehovot.

31. Gilbert N Lewis (1875-1946)

Gilbert Newton Lewis was an American chemist born in 1875 at Weymouth to Frank Wesley Lewis. He was a former dean of the college of chemistry at the University of California. He is remembered for his theory of valence bond theory on chemical bonding. Besides, he contributed to chemical thermodynamics, photochemistry and isotope separation. In 1926, he coined the term "photon" for the smallest unit of radient energy.

He received Ph.D from the Harvard Univesity. He studied in Germany as well. Later, he moved to University of California, where he served as dean of college of chemistry.

He conducted research on measurement of free energies of several chemical processes. In 1916, he proposed his theory of bonding. He started work on isotope separation in 1933. As a consequence, he was able to separate a sample of heavy water. He developed theory of acids and bases. Later, he worked on photochemistry for the rest of his life.

He died in 1946 at Berkeley laboratory because of hydrogen cyanide poisoning.

32. Karl Theophil Fries (1875 – 1962)

Karl Theophil Fries was a German chemist born in 1875 at Kiedrich. He studied chemistry at the University of Marburg under Theodor Zincke. He served as professor of chemistry in Marburg. He took part in the World War I. Later, he became professor at the Technical University at Brunswick. He forced to retire in 1938 by Nazis. He went back to Marburg for teaching.

He is notable for the discovery of Fries rearrangement in organic synthesis.

He died in 1962 at Marburg.

33. Heinrich Houben (1875 - 1940)

Heinrich Hubert Maria Josef Houben was a German chemist born in 1875 at Waldfeucht. He worked on ketone, terpene and camphor synthesis. He served as head of war laboratory in World War I. He improved the Hoesch reaction; today it is called as Houben-Hoesch reaction.

He studied at the University of Bonn under August Kekulé. He received doctoral degree in 1898 under Julius Bredt. After working at the University of Aachen and the University of Bonn, he joined the laboratory of Emil Fischer at the University of Berlin. After the war, he became professor at the Biologische Reichsanstalt in Berlin Dahlem in 1921.

He died in 1940 at Tübingen.

34. Erik C Clemmensen (1876 – 1941)

Erik Christian Clemmensen was a Danish-American chemist born in 1876 at Odense. He is well kown for his Clemmensen reduction, where keto group is reduced into methylene group.

He studied at the Copenhagen Polytechnic Institute. He emigrated to the United States in 1900 and workd on pharmaceutical chemistry. He received Ph.D for the invention of Clemmensen reduction in 1913 from the University of Copenhagen.

In 1914, he co-founded the Commonwealth chemical corporation in New York, where he developed methods for the manufacture of sodium benzoate, vanillin and coumarin. After a fire in 1929, this company was acquired by Monsanto Chemical Company. During his work at Monsanto, he helped to develop the synthesis of artificial sweetener.

In 1935, he returned to New York and founded The Clemmensen Chemical Corp.

He died in 1941 at Newark, New York.

35. Adolf Windaus (1876 – 1959)

Adolf Otto Reinhold Windaus was a German chemist born in 1876 at Berlin. He was married to Elizabeth Resau in 1915. He received the Nobel Prize in Chemistry for his work on sterols and their relation with vitamins. He received the Goethe Medal as well.

He studied at the University of Berlin and the University of Freiburg. He served as the head of the chemical institute at the University of Göttingen. He was one of the chemists who did not work with Nazis. He declined to do research on poison gas (chemical warfare) during World War I.

He died in 1959 at Göttingen.

36. Alfred Stock (1876 – 1946)

Alfred Stock was a German chemist born in 1876 at Danzig. He worked on hydrides of boron and silicon, coordination chemistry, mercury and mercury poisoning.

He studied at the Friedrich Wilhelm University in Berlin. He got Ph.D degree on quantitative separation of arsenic and antimony. He worked as professor at the University of Breslau. He served as director of the Kaiser Wilhelm Institute for Chemistry and chemistry department at the Technische Hochschule in Karlsruhe. He was a visiting professor at Cornell University, New York.

He died in 1946 at Aken an der Elbe.

The German Chemical Society's Alfred-Stock Memorial Prize is named after him.

37. Otto Diels (1876 – 1954)

Otto Paul Hermann Diels was a German chemist born in 1876 at Hamburg. One of his notable works was Diels-Alder reaction with Kurt Alder. They received the Nobel Prize in Chemistry in 1850 for their work. This method has valuable applications in the synthesis of synthetic rubber and plastic.

He studied at the University of Berlin. He studied chemistry under Emil Fischer. He worked at the University of Kiel.

He died in 1954 at Kiel.

38. Frederick Soddy (1877 –1956)

Frederick Soddy was an English chemist born in 1877 at Eastbourne to Benjamin Soddy and Hannah Green. He explained with Ernest Rutherford about transmutation of elements in radioactivity. He proved the existence of isotopes of some radioactive elements. He was a master in chemistry, statistical mechanics, finance and economics.

He was educated at Eastbourne College, University college of Wales and at Merton college. He was graduated in 1898. He was a researcher at Oxford between 1898 and 1900.

In 1900, he was a demonstrator in chemistry at McGill University, where he worked with Rutherford on radioactivity. In 1903, he with Sir William Ramsay proved the decay of radium produced helium gas. Between 1904 and 1914, he was a lecturer at the University of Glasgow. In 1910, he was elected as a fellow of the Royal Society. In 1914, he was appointed to a chair at the University of Anerdeen, where he worked on research related to the World War I. He received the Nobel Prize in Chemistry in 1921. He died in 1956 at Brighton.

39. Francis W Aston (1877 – 1945)

Francis William Aston was an English chemist and physicist born in 1877 at Harborne to William Aston and Fanny Charlotte Hollis. He received the Nobel Prize in Chemistry in 1922 for the discovery of non-radioactive elements by mass spectrograph. He was a fellow of the Royal Society and fellow of Trinity College.

He was educated at the Harborne Vicarage School, Malvern College, and Mason College. In a private laboratory he conducted research on organic chemistry. In 1898, he worked on optical properties of tartaric acid compounds at Frankland. Later, he worked on fermentation chemistry at Birmingham. He was employed at W. Butler & Co. Brewery in 1900.

He got scholarship from the University of Birmingham to conduct research on X-rays and radioactivity. He studied current through a gas-filled tube. He conducted research with self-made discharge tubes, which led to the discovery of Aston dark space.

He travelled across the globe in 1908. In 1909, he was appointed as lecturer at the University of Birmingham. In 1910, he moved to the Cavendish laboratory in Cambridge on invitation by J. J. Thomson.

He worked on the identification of isotopes of the elements neon, chlorine and mercury. The World War I delayed most of his research. He worked at the Royal Aircraft Establishment as technical assistant on aeronautical coatings. After the war, he returned to the Cavendish Laboratory and completed construction of mass spectrograph.

He became a member of the International Committee on Atomic Weights, fellow of the Royal Society. He won the Nobel Prize in Chemistry in 1922.

He died in 1945 at Cambridge at the age of 68.

40. Heinrich Otto Wieland (1877 – 1957)

Heinrich Otto Wieland was a German chemist born in 1877 at Pforzheim to Theodor Wieland. He received the Nobel Prize in Chemistry in 1927 for his research on bile acids.

He received his doctoral degree form the University of Munich under the supersion of Johannes Thiele. In 1914, he was appointed as associate professor and director of the State Laboratory of Munich. Between 1917 and 1918, he worked at Kaiser Wilhelm Institute for Physical Chemistry and Electrochemistry for military service. He worked here on synthetic routes for mustard gas. He was the first to synthesize Adamsite.

Between 1913 and 1921, he was a professor at the Technical University of Munich. Later, he moved to University of Freiburg, where he worked on toad poisons and bile acids. With Boehringer Ingelheim, he worked on total synthesis of morphine and strychnine. In 1825, he succeeded Richard Willstätter as professor of chemistry at the University of Munich.

In 1941, he isolated the toxin α-amanitin from the world'd most poisonous mushrooms Amanita phalloides. He protected Jewish people who were racially burdened.

Since 1964, the Heinrich Wieland Prize is being given in his honor. He was the first to promote research on chemistry, biochemistry, physiology and medicine.

He died in 1957 at Starnberg.

41. Franz J Emil Fischer (1877–1947)

Franz Joseph Emil Fischer was a German chemist born in 1877 at Freiburg. He was the founder of the Kaiser Wilhelm Institute for Coal Research. He is well known for the discovery of the Fischer-Tropsch process.

He produced liquid hydrocarbons from carbon monoxide and hydrogen in the presence of metal catalyst at 150-300°C. He worked with Wilhelm Ostwald and Hermann Emil Fischer.

He died in 1947 at Munich.

42. Julius Nieuwland (1878 – 1936)

Julius Aloysius (Arthur) Nieuwland was a Belgian-born chemist born in 1878. He was a priest, professor of chemistry and botany at the University of Notre Dame. He worked more on acetylene, which was used in a kind of synthetic rubber. During this work, he discovered neoprene.

He studied at the University of Notre Dame and the Catholic University of America. He worked on acetylene chemistry during his doctoral degree study. At this time, he discovered the chemical lewisite, which was a chemical warfare agent. He was hospitalized for several days during this research. He received Ph.D in 1904.

He was appointed as professor of chemistry at the Notre Dame. He founded American Midland Naturalist and hewas its editor until 1934. In 1920, he polymerized acetylene into divinylacetylene.

He died in 1936 at the age of 58.

43. Johannes N Brønsted (1879-1947)

Johannes Nicolaus Brønsted was a Danish chemist born in 1879 at Varde. He developed acid-base theory.

In 1897, he started his study at the Polytechnique Institute in Copenhagen and also studied at the University of Copenhagen. He received Ph.D degree in 1908. Later, he became professor at the University of Copenhagen.

In 1929, he was a visiting professor at Yale University. He was nominated four times for Nobel Prize. He was a fellow of the Royal Society and member of the National Academy of Sciences. In his early career, he studied chemical thermodynamics and later electrolyte solutions. He worked more on reaction kinetics. In 1923, he identified that acid-base reactions involved the transfer of a proton. Proton is transferred by the acid to the base. Meanwhile, the British chemist Martin Lowry also proposed the same theory.

He died in 1947 at Copenhagen.

44. Hans Meerwein (1879–1965)

Hans Meerwein was a German chemist born in 1879 at Hamburg to Wilhelm Emil Meerwein. He is well known for Meerwein–Ponndorf–Verley reduction, Wagner–Meerwein rearrangement, Meerwein arylation and Meerwein's salt.

He studied at Fresenius University of Applied Sciences and at the University of Bonn. He was awarded the Ph.D degree under Richard Anschütz. He started his career at the University of Berlin. He was a professor at the University of Königsberg. Finally, he worked at the University of Marburg.

He died in 1965 at Marburg.

45. Otto Hahn (1879 – 1968)

Otto Hahn was a German chemist born in 1879 at Frankfurt am Main. His research areas include radioactivity and radiochemistry. He is considered as father of nuclear chemistry. He with Lise Meitner discovered isotopes of radium, thorium, protactinium and uranium. Thus, he discoved the phenomenon of nuclear isomerism. He developed rubidium-strontium dating. In 1938, He with Lise Meitner and Fritz Strassmann discovered nuclear fission. He received the Nobel Prize in Chemistry in 1944.

He studied at the University of Marburg, University College London with William Ramsay and McGill University under Ernest Rutherford.

He faught in World War I on behalf of Germany. He worked with Fritz Haber for chemical warfare.

After the war, he became the head of the Kaiser Wilhelm Institute for Chemistry. He worked with Strassmann and Meitner on bombardment of uranium and thorium by neutron, which led to the discovery of nuclear fission.

During World War II, he worked on the German nuclear weapons program. As a result, he was arrested by the Allied forces and imprisoned with nine other German scientists until 1946.

He served as the last president of the Kaiser Wilhelm Society for the Advancement of Science and he was the founder president of Max Planck Society between 1948 and 1960. In 1950, he was instrumental in the establishment of Federation of German Scientists. He worked hard to rebuild the German science after world war II.

He died in 1968 at Göttingen.

46. Henry Drysdale Dakin (1880 – 1952)

Henry Drysdale Dakin was an English chemist born in 1880 at London. He was married to Christian Herter in 1916. He studied at the University of Leeds with Julius B Cohen, at the University of Heidelberg with Albrecht Kossel and the Columbia University in 1905 with Christian Herter. In 1905, he successfuly synthesized adrenaline in the laboratoty.

He worked as a chemist with Alexis Carrel for the Rockefeller Institute. They developed the Carrel-Dakin method for wound treatments, which consists of soaking of wounds with sodium hypochlorite and boric acid. He later developed Dakin reaction and Dakin-West reaction.

He died in 1952 at Scarsdale, New York.

47. Claude Silbert Hudson (1881 – 1952)

Claude Silbert Hudson was an American chemist born in 1881 at Atlanta. He worked on carbohydrate chemistry. In 1901, he was graduated from the Princeton University. He studied under Walther Nernst and Jacobus Henricus van't Hoff in Europe.

After his return to United States, he worked as an instructor of physics at the Princeton University and then at the University of Illinois. He received doctoral degree from this university in 1907. Later, he held positions at the National Bureau of Standards and the NIH. He is remembered for Hudson's rules in carbohydrate chemistry.

Claude S. Hudson Award is given in carbohydrate chemistry by American Chemical Society in his honor. In 1927, he was elected to the National Academy of Science. In 1942, he was awarded the Elliott Cresson Medal and, in 1929, Willard Gibbs Award. He died in 1952.

48. Irving Langmuir (1881-1957)

Irving Langmuir was an American chemist born in 1881 at Brooklyn to Charles Langmuir and Sadie. In 1932, he won the Nobel Prize in Chemistry for his work on surface chemistry. He proposed 'concentric theory of atomic structure'. He developed gas-filled incandescent lamp and hydrogen welding technique.

He studied in many schools and institutes between 1892 and 1895 in America and Paris. He received B.Sc. degree in metallurgical engineering from the Columbia University School of Mines in 1903. In 1906, he received Ph.D degree on 'On the Partial Recombination of Dissolved Gases during Cooling' under the supervision of Friedrich Dolezalek in Göttingen.

Later, he taught at Stevens Institute of Technology in Hoboken, New Jersey until 1909. Then he worked for General Electric research laboratory.

He died in 1957 at Woods Hole at the age of 76.

49. Hans Fischer (1881 – 1945)

Hans Fischer was a German chemist born in 1881 at Höchst on Main to Eugen Fischer and Anna Herdegen. In 1930, he received the Nobel Prize in Chemistry for his work on synthesis of haemin.

He studied chemistry and medicine at the University of Lausanne and the University of Marburg. He started his work at a Medical Clinic in Munich and then at the First Berlin Chemical Institute. In 1913, he became lecturer in physiology. In 1916, he became professor of medical chemistry at the University of Innsbruck. He moved to the University of Vienna in 1918. He was a professor of organic chemistry at the Technical University of Munich. He died in 1945 at Munich.

50. Hermann Staudinger (1881 –1965)

Hermann Staudinger was a German chemist born in 1881 at Worms. He identified macromolecules as polymers. For this work, he received the Nobel Prize in Chemistry in 1953. He is well known for the discovery of ketenes and Staudinger reaction. He with Leopold Ružička elucidated the molecular structures of pyrethrin I and II. He later developed pyrethroid insecticides.

Initially, he wanted to become a botanist, but studied chemistry at the University of Halle, at the TH Darmstadt and at the LMU Munich. In 1903, he received doctoral degree from the University of Halle. In 1907, he qualified as an academic lecturer at the University of Strasbourg.

He died in 1965 at Freiburg.

51. Walter N Haworth (1883-1950)

Sir Walter Norman Haworth was a British chemist born in 1883 at White Coppice. He is well known for his work on ascorbic acid (Vitamin C). He received the Nobel Prize in Chemistry in 1937 for his investigations on carbohydrates and vitamin C. He worked to elucidate correct structure of many sugars. He developed Haworth projection formulae.

He studied at the University of Manchester and the University of Göttingen. In 1912, he became a lecturer at United College of University of St Andrews. He developed methods for the production chemicals and drugs for the British government during World War I.

He became professor of chemistry at the Armstrong College and then at the University of Birmingham. He deduced the structures of maltose, cellobiose, melibiose, gentiobiose, raffinose and glucoside.

He died in 1950 at Barnt Green.

52. Peter J W Debye (1884 – 1966)

Peter Joseph William Debye was a Dutch-American chemist born in 1884 at Maastricht. He received Nobel Prize in Chemistry.

He studied at the Aachen University of Technology under Arnold Sommerfeld. He completed electrical engineering in 1905. He worked on radiation pressure for his doctoral thesis. He derived Planck radiation formula in 1910.

He was a professor at the University of Zurich. He then moved to Utrecht in 1912, to Göttingen in 1913, ETH Zurich in 1920, to University of Leipzig in 1927 and to Berlin in 1934.

He became a member of the Royal Netherlands Academy of Arts and Sciences in 1914.

He developed equations relating dipole moments to temperature and dielectric constant. Later, he extended Einstein theory of specific heat to lower temperatures by incorporating contributions from low-frequency phonons. In 1913, he extended the theory of atomic structure into elliptical orbits, which was also introduced by Arnold Sommerfeld. He calculated the effect of temperature on X-ray diffraction. He improved theory of electrical conductivity in electrolyte solutions. He developed a theory to explain the Compton effect.

Between 1934 and 1939, he was the director of physics section of Kaiser Wilhelm Institute. Later, he was a professor of physics at the Frederick William University. He visited Cornell University in United States and became a professor there. In 1946, he became citizen of America. He retired in 1952. Most of his works in USA were based on light scattering techniques and determination of molecular weight of polymers.

He died in 1966 because of heart attack at Ithaca.

53. Friedrich K R Bergius (1884 – 1949)

Friedrich Karl Rudolf Bergius was a German chemist born in 1884 at Breslau. He is well known for the Bergius process for the production of fuel from coal. He received the Nobel Prize in Chemistry in 1931 for his work on high pressure chemistry. After World War II, he settled in Argentina.

He studied at the University of Breslau and received doctoral degree from University of Leipzig in 1907. He worked with Fritz Haber and Carl Bosch at the University of Karlsruhe for the development of Haber-Bosch process. He joined Leibniz University Hannover as a professor and developed the idea of chemical kinetics.

He died in 1949 at Buenos Aires.

54. Theodor Svedberg (1884 – 1971)

Theodor Svedberg was a Swedish chemist born in 1884 at Fleräng to Augusta Alstermark and Elias Svedberg. He received the Nobel Prize in Chemistry in 1926 for his work on colloids and proteins using the ultracentrifuge.

He studied and worked at the Uppsala University until 1949. Later, he was in charge of the Gustaf Werner Institute until 1967.

He was a foreign member of the Royal Society in 1944 and he was a part of the National Academy of Sciences in 1945.

He died in 1971 at Kopparberg.

55. George A L Sarton (1884 – 1956)

George Alfred Leon Sarton was a Belgian-born American chemist and historian born at Ghent to Léonie Van Halmé and Alfred Sarton. He is the founder of the discipline 'history of science'.

He studied at the University of Ghent. He received many honors. He received his doctoral degree in 1911 on celestial mechanics. During World War I, he was migrated to England *via* the Netherlands. Later, he went to America. He taught at the University of Illinois. He lectured at Harvard University and became a lecturer there at 1920. Later, he was a professor of history of science from 1940 to 1951.

He died in 1956 at Cambridge.

56. Chika Kuroda (1884 – 1968)

Chika Kuroda was a Japanese chemist born in 1884 at Saga Prefecture. She worked on natural pigments. She was the first woman, who received B.Sc. degree in Japan.

She worked in many schools. She admitted to Tohoku Imperial University. She was monitored by Prof. Riko Majima, who inspired her to study organic chemistry. She worked on natural pigments. She completed her bachelor degree in 1916.

She was appointed as assistant professor at Tohoku Imperial University. Later, she became professor at Tokyo Women's Higher Normal School in 1918. She was the first woman to give presentation at the Chemical Society of Japan. She visited University of Oxford in 1921, where she worked with William Henry Perkin. In 1924, she was invited by RIKEN institute to conduct research on carthamin (a pigment in safflower plants). She received her doctoral degree in 1929 on 'The Constitution of Carthamin'. She died in 1968.

57. Fritz Arndt (1885-1969)

Fritz Georg Arndt was a German chemist born in 1885 at Hamburg. He is a well known synthetic organic chemist. He was married with Julia Heimann in 1914. He with Bernd Eistert discovered the Arndt-Eistert synthesis.

He studied at the University of Geneva and the University of Bern. He received doctoral degree in 1908 from the University of Freiburg by working with Ludwig Gattermann.

He started short term work at the University of Greifswald, University of Kiel and University of Breslau. In 1915, he was appointed to the chair of chemistry at the University of Istanbul. Later, he returned to the University of Breslau. In 1933, his office was abandoned by Nazi government.

He visited Oxford University and went back to Istanbul where he stayed from 1934 to 1955. He is influencial for the development of chemistry in Turkey. In 1955, he returned to the University of Hamburg, Germany.

He died in 1969 at Hamburg.

58. Max Volmer (1885 – 1965)

Max Volmer was a German chemist born in 1885 at Hilden. He is well known for his contributions to electrochemistry. He with Butler developed Butler-Volmer equation. He was the director of the Physical Chemistry and Electrochemistry Institute of the Technische Hochschule Berlin.

After World War II, he went to the Soviet Union as head of bureau for the production of heavy water. He retuned to East Germany after ten years as professor at the Humboldt University of Berlin. He was the president of the East German Academy of Sciences.

He died in 1965 at Potsdam.

59. Satoyasu Iimori (1885 – 1982)

Satoyasu Iimori was a Japanese chemist born in 1885 at Kanazawa. He was a pioneer of radiochemistry. He is considered as the father of radiation chemistry in Japan.

He studied at Tokyo Imperial University and graduate college of the university. In 1917, he worked on analysis of various minerals at Institute of Physical and Chemical Research (RIKEN). In 1919, he went to UK and studied at the Cambridge University. He worked under Soddy from 1920 on radiochemistry. After his return to Japan, he became the chief researcher of RIKEN, where he worked on radiochemistry, analytical chemistry, photochemistry and geochemistry.

During World War II, he contributed for the search of uranium ore. He was a member of the RIKEN, Chemical Society of Japan and Society of the Analytical Chemistry of Japan. After his retirement, he became interested in the synthesis of artificial gemstones.

He died in 1982 at Toshima-ku Sugamo.

60. George Hevesy (1885 – 1966)

George Charles de Hevesy was a Hungarian chemist born in 1885 at Budapest. He received Nobel Prize in Chemistry in 1943 for his work on development of radioactive tracers in the study of metabolic reactions in animals. He was also the co-discoverer of the element hafnium.

He studied at the University of Budapest, Technical University of Berlin and University of Freiburg. He received his doctoral degree in 1908. He worked with with Fritz Haber, Ernest Rutherford and Niels Bohr. Later, he was appointed as professor in 1918. In 1920, he settled in Copenhagen.

He died in 1966 at Freiburg.

61. Robert Robinson (1886 – 1975)

Sir Robert Robinson was a British chemist born in 1886 at Derbyshire to James Bradbury Robinson and Jane Davenport. He received Nobel Prize in Chemistry in 1947 for his work on plant dyestuffs and alkaloids.

He studied at the University of Manchester. Later, he was appointed as professor at the University of Sydney in 1912. Between 1912 and 1920, he worked at St Andrews University. Later, he worked at Manchester University, University College London and Oxford University.

He died in 1975 at Great Missenden.

62. Kazimierz Fajans (1887 –1975)

Kazimierz Fajans was a Polish American chemist born in 1887 at Warsaw. He worked on radioactivity and discovered protactinium.

He studied at the University of Leipzig, Heidelberg and Zürich. He received doctoral degree in 1909 on stereoselective synthesis of chiral compounds.

In 1910, he joined Ernest Rutherford laboratory. He returned to Germany and became assistant professor at Technical University of Karlsruhe. Later, he joined Munich University. In 1932, he became the head of physical chemistry at Rockefeller Foundation. In 1935, he left Germany because of escalation of Nazi persecution. He stayed in Cambridge for sometime and then migrated to the University of Michigan.

He was an honorary member of the Polish Chemical Society.

He died in 1975 at Ann Arbor.

63. Akira Ogata (1887 - 1978)

Akira Ogata was a Japanese chemist born in 1887 at Osaka. He is well known for the first synthesis of methamphetamine in 1919.

He studied at the University of Tokyo and Humboldt University of Berlin. In 1920, he became professor at the University of Tokyo.

He died in 1978.

64. James Batcheller Sumner (1887 – 1955)

James Batcheller Sumner was an American chemist born in 1887 at Canton. He received the Nobel Prize in Chemistry in 1946 for the discovery of crystallization of enzymes. He was the first to prove that enzymes are proteins.

He studied at the Harvard University in 1910. He taught at Mount Allison University, Canada. In 1912, he went to Harvard Medical School to study biochemistry. He was a professor of biochemistry at Cornell Medical School.

He died in 1955 at Buffalo.

65. Leopold Ružička (1887 – 1976)

Leopold Ružička was a Croatian-Swiss chemist born in 1887 at Vukovar. He won the Nobel Prize in Chemistry in 1939 for his work on polymethylenes, higher terpenes and synthesis of male sex hormones. He was a recipient of eight *honoris causa* in science. He had twenty four memberships in chemical, biochemical and other scientific societies.

He obtained his doctoral degree in 1910.

He died in 1976 at Mammern, Switzerland.

66. Paul Karrer (1889 – 1971)

Paul Karrer was a Swiss chemist born in 1889 at Moscow. He worked on vitamins. He was married to Helena Froelich in 1914. He received the Nobel Prize in Chemistry in 1937.

He studied at the University of Zurich under Alfred Werner and received Ph.D degree in 1911. He worked as an assistant in the Chemical Institute. In 1919, he became professor of chemistry and director of the Chemical Institute.

He worked on metal complexes and plant pigments (carotenoids). He demonstrated that these carotenoids are converted into vitamin A in the body. He confirmed the structure of ascorbic acid (vitamin C). He extended his research into vitamin B_2 and E.

He published many articles and received many honours and awards.

He died in 1971 at Zürich.

67. Jaroslav Heyrovský (1890 – 1967)

Jaroslav Heyrovský was a Czechoslovakian chemist born in 1890 at Prague to Leopold Heyrovský. He invented polarographic method. He is considered as the father of electroanalytical methods. In 1959, he received the Nobel Prize in Chemistry for his work on development of polarographic methods of analysis.

He studied at the Charles University in Prague. Between 1910 and 1914, he studied under William Ramsay at the University College London. During World War I, he worked in a military hospital as dispensing chemist and radiologist. He completed his doctoral degree in 1918 and D.Sc. in London in 1921.

He died in 1967 at Prague.

68. John H Northrop (1891 – 1987)

John Howard Northrop was an American biochemist born in 1891 at Yonkerslice to Alice Rich Northrop. He won the Nobel Prize in Chemistry in 1946 for his work on isolation, crystallization, study of enzymes, proteins and viruses. He worked at Rockefeller Institute for Medical Research in New York.

He was educated at the Columbia University. He received doctoral degree in 1915. During World War I, he worked for U. S. Chemical Warfare on production of acetone and ethanol through fermentation. This work led to study enzymes. He isolated, crystallized and characterized gastric enzyme pepsin, the first bacteriophage, pepsinogen, trypsin, chymotrypsin and carboxy peptidase.

He died in 1987 at Wickenburg.

69. Alice Augusta Ball (1892 – 1916)

Alice Augusta Ball was an American chemist born in 1892 at Seattle to James Presley and Laura Louise (Howard) Ball. She developed 'Ball Method' for the treatment of leprosy. She was the first African American to receive master's degree from the University of Hawaii. She was also the universities first female and African American professor.

She studied at the University of Washington. She published a work 'Benzoylations in ether solution' in Journal of the American Chemical Society. This was an uncommon accomplishment by a woman. She received offers from many colleges and universities for master's degree. She joined College of Hawaii and worked on chemical properties of the Kava plant species. Later, Harry T. Hollmann guided her to study chaulmoogra oil.

He died in 1916 at Seattle.

70. Homer Burton Adkins (1892–1949)

Homer Burton Adkins was an American chemist born in 1892 at Newport to Emily (née Middleswart) and Alvin Adkins. He worked on hydrogenation of organic compounds. He worked during World War II on chemical agents and poisonous gases.

He studied at Denison University and Ohio State University. He received his doctoral degree in 1918. He worked for United States Department of War. Later, he worked as an instructor at Ohio State University. In 1919, he came to the University of Wisconsin–Madison. He worked for Bakelite Corporation in summer of 1924 and 1926. He was the director of the National Defence Research Committee.

He conducted research on rates of oxidation of acetaldehyde and oxalic acid by potassium permanganate, cycloaddition of oxides on esters. He used copper chromite for the hydrogenation of ester to an alcohol. He continued experiments on hydrogenation. He published many books. His laboratory at Wisconsin focused on chemical warfare research. He also studied on development of chemicals and ointments to remove effects of poisonous agents. He received Medal for Merit in 1948 in recognition of his work.

He died in 1949 at St. Louis.

71. Johannes Martin Bijvoet (1892 – 1980)

Johannes Martin Bijvoet was a Dutch chemist born in 1892 at Amsterdam. He is well known for the establishment of absolute configuration of molecules. He worked with van't Hoff on tetrahedrally bound carbon.

In 1946, he became a member of the Royal Netherlands Academy of Arts and Sciences.

He died in 1980 at Winterswijk.

72. James Bryant Conant (1893 − 1978)

James Bryant Conant was an American chemist born in 1893 at Dorchester. His contributions are remembered as president of Harvard University and the first U.S. Ambassador to West Germany.

He received doctoral degree from Harvard in 1916. During World War I, he worked for U.S. Army on the development of poisonous gases. He joined Harvard University in 1919 and became professor in 1929. He worked on structural elucidation of natural products particularly chlorophyll. He determined the complex relationship between chemical equilibrium and reaction rate. He investigated the biochemistry of oxyhemoglobin. He also contributed to modern theories of acid-base chemistry. In 1925, he visited Germany for eight months. He met many leading chemists - Theodor Curtius, Kazimierz Fajans, Hans Fischer, Arthur Hantzsch, Hans Meerwein, Jakob Meisenheimer, Hermann Staudinger and Karl Ziegler.

He became the president of the Harvard University in 1933. Later, he was appointed to the National Defence Research Committee in 1940. He worked on development of synthetic rubber and Manhattan Project, which developed the first atomic bomb. After the war, he worked for Joint Research and Development Board.

He wrote books on scientific method to laymen. He published 55 research articles between 1928 and 1933. In 1953, he retired from Harvard and became the United States High Commissioner for Germany. He published his autobiography '*My Several Lives*' in 1970.

He died in 1978 at Hanover.

73. Harold Clayton Urey (1893 – 1981)

Harold Clayton Urey was an American chemist born in 1893 at Walkerton. He worked on isotopes. He won the Nobel Prize in Chemistry in 1934 for the discovery of deuterium. He was involved in the development of atom bomb. He contributed to theories on the development of organic life from non-living matter.

He studied thermodynamics under Gilbert Lewis at the University of California, Berkeley. In 1923, he received his doctoral degree. He also studied at the Niels Bohr Institute in Copenhagen under a fellowship by the American-Scandinavian Foundation. He was a research associate at Johns Hopkins University. Later, he became associate professor at Columbia University. In 1931, he started work on separation of isotopes, which resulted in the discovery of deuterium.

During World War II, he utilized his knowledge of isotope separation to enrich uranium. He headed the group at Columbia University to seperate uranium isotope by gas diffusion. After the war, he became professor at the Institute for Nuclear Studies. Later, he joined University of Chicago as professor.

He postulated that early terrestrial atmosphere was composed of ammonia, methane and hydrogen. His student Stanley L Miller demonstrated the formation of amino acids when mixture of these gases was exposed to electric spark with water. This experiment is popular as Miller–Urey experiment.

He shifted to University of California, San Diego as professor. In later years, he became interested in space science when Apollo 11 returned with moon's rock samples.

He died in 1981 at La Jolla.

74. Christopher K Ingold (1893 – 1970)

Sir Christopher Kelk Ingold was a British chemist born in 1893 at London. He is well known for the introduction of concepts like nucleophile, electrophile, inductive and resonance effects. He was also a co-author of Cahn-Ingold-Prelog rules. He is considered as one of the pioneers of physical organic chemistry.

He studied at Hartley University College at Southampton, University of London. He worked under Jocelyn Field Thorpe at Imperial College, London. He worked during World War I for the development of poison gas. He received doctoral degree in 1918 and D. Sc. in 1921. In 1924, he shifted to the University of Leeds. He returned to London in 1930 to work at University College London. He discovered S_N1, S_N2, E1 and E2 mechanisms.

He was knighted in 1958. He died in 1970 at Edgware.

75. Henry Gilman (1893 – 1986)

Henry Gilman was an American chemist born in 1893 at Boston. He is considered as the father of organometallic chemistry. He discovered the Gilman reagent.

He was educated in Harvard University and completed Ph. D degree in 1918. He met Madam Curie and Victor Grignard in Europe. He joined University of Illinois as associate professor. Later, he shifted to Iowa State College.

During World War II, he was involved in Manhattan Project. In 1947, he suffered from glaucoma and lost his one eye.

He died in 1986 at Ames. Chemistry building at Iowa State University is renamed as Henry Gilman Hall in his memory.

76. Leonora Bilger (1893 – 1975)

Leonora Bilger was an American chemist born in 1893 at Boston to George Neuffer and Elizabeth Neuffer. She worked on nitrogen compounds. She is notable as a teacher and administrator at the University of Hawaii.

She studied at the University of Cincinnati and got her doctoral degree in 1916. She started work at Sweet Briar College. She moved to alma mater's department of chemistry, where she worked for ten years. She spent a year at Newnham College Cambridge University. Then, she moved to University of Hawaii with her husband.

She worked on nitrogenous compounds. At Cincinnati, she worked on asymmetric nitrogenous compounds. She continued her research at Hawaii. She also worked on anti-cancer compounds. She examined sterols in tropical oils and pigments in red peppers.

She died in 1975.

77. Francis Simon (1893 –1956)

Sir Francis Simon was a German-British chemist born in 1893 at Berlin to Ernst Simon and Anna Mendelssohn. He formulated the gaseous diffusion method, which was used for the enrichment of uranium-235 isotope. He majorly contributed to the development of atomic bomb. In World War I, he won the Iron Cross First Class.

He studied at the University of Berlin under Walther Nernst on low-temperature physics related to third law of thermodynamics (Nernst heat theorem). In 1931, he joined University of Breslau as professor.

Because of fascism in Germany, he then migrated to UK by starting work at University of Oxford. He liquified helium in 1936. In the same year, he was appointed as reader to University of Oxford.

He died in 1956 at Oxford.

78. Jnanendra Nath Mukherjee (1893 – 1983)

Jnanendra Nath Mukherjee was an Indian chemist born in 1893 at Rajshahi (now in Bangladesh) to Durgadas Mukherjee and Shrimati Saratshashi Devi. He worked on colloids.

He studied at Presidency College and received B.Sc. and M.Sc. in 1913 and 1915 respectively from Rajabazar Science College. He published electric synthesis of colloids for his M.Sc. thesis in the Journal of the American Chemical Society in 1915.

In 1919, he joined the University College, London to work in the physical chemistry laboratory under Donnan. He continued his research on colloids. His major concern was to develop theory of the electrokinetic double layer and its ionic constitution. He is well known for the development of boundary method for the determination of cataphoretic speed of colloidal particles.

He had the visualization about how basic soil colloid studies are useful in understanding soil properties and problems. In 1942, he developed a rotary viscometer for the study of anomalous viscous properties. In 1944, he developed the method of crude oils based on chromatography capillary analysis and fluorescence in UV light.

He played a main role in the development of agricultural research and education in the country. In 1945, he became the director of the Imperial (now Indian Agricultural Research Institute, New Delhi). He reorganised the research and educational activities of this Institute and in the whole country as well. Under his direction, this institute expanded academic activities. He is responsible for the initiation of research on soil-plant studies. He created divisions like Soil Survey, Soil Physics, Agricultural Chemistry, Soil Fertility, Soil Microbiology, Biochemistry, Organic Chemistry and Spectroscopy in soil science.

He died in 1983 at Calcutta.

79. Jnan Chandra Ghosh (1894 –1959)

Jnan Chandra Ghosh was an Indian chemist born in 1894 at Giridih to Ram Chandra Ghosh. He is remembered for his contribution to the development of scientific research, industrial development and technology education in India. He was the director of Eastern Higher Technical Institute (now IIT Kharagpur) in 1950. He was the director of Indian Institute of Science and Vice Chancellor of University of Calcutta. He worked on strong electrolytes and dissociation-ionization theory, study of photocatalysts and differential thermal analysis.

He enrolled in Presidency College, Calcutta. He was influenced by Acharya Prafulla Chandra Ray. He was appointed as lecturer at Rajabazar Science College. He travelled to UK to pursue Ph.D degree at the University College of Science in London. He got recognition from Max Planck, William Bragg and Walther Nernst. He was awarded D.Sc. degree for his work on strong electrolytes. During his stay in UK, he worked under Frederick G. Donnan for sometime.

In 1921, he returned to India and started work at newly established Dacca University as professor and head of the department of chemistry. He worked there for twenty years. During this time, he contributed to photo-chemistry, bio-chemistry and agricultural chemistry. He made people to study science by his devotion and personality.

In 1939, he got a call to succeed C V Raman as the Director of the Indian Institute of Science at Bangalore. In 1943, he was knighted for his war services.

He was committed for the development of industries in India. He served as Director-General of Industry and Supply from 1947 to 1950. In 1954, the Government of India awarded him Padma Bhushan in recognition of his ability and service to the country.

He died in 1959 at Calcutta.

80. Izzal Kolthoff (1894-1993)

Izaak Maurits Kolthoff was a Dutch-born American chemist born in 1894 at Almelo. He is considered as the father of analytical chemistry. He developed the cold process for the production of synthetic rubber. He was active in social causes like promoting world peace and opposing nuclear weapons testing.

He worked under Nicholas Schoorl. Nicholas introduced electro-analytical chemistry and co-precipitation to Kolthoff. He received the Ph.D degree from the University of Utrecht. In 1927, he joined to the University of Minnesota, United States.

He died in 1993 at St. Paul, Minnesota.

81. Shanti Swaroop Bhatnagar (1894 –1955)

Shanti Swaroop Bhatnagar was an Indian chemist born in 1894 at Bhera to Parmeshwari Sahai Bhatnagar. He was an academician and scientific administrator. He was the first director-general of the Council of Scientific and Industrial Research (CSIR). He is considered as the father of research

laboratories in India. He was also the first chairman of the University Grants Commission (UGC).

His father died when he was only eight months old. He was educated by his grandfather. In 1911, he joined Dayal Singh College, Lahore (now in New Delhi). He received B.Sc. and M.Sc. from Forman Christian College in 1916 and 1919 respectively. In 1921, he received doctorate in science from University College London under Professor Frederick G. Donnan. On retuning to to India, he joined newly established Banaras Hindu University as professor.

He died in 1955 at New Delhi.

82. Margaret Dorothy Foster (1895 – 1970)

Margaret Dorothy Foster was an American chemist born in 1895 at Chicago to James Edward Foster and Minnie Foster. She was the first scientist to work in United States Geological Survey. She was recruited to work on the Manhattan Project.

She was graduated from Illinois College, George Washington University and American University with a doctoral degree.

During geological survey, she worked on detection of minerals from naturally occurring bodies of water. In 1942, she worked for the Manhattan Project under Roger C. Wells for the development of quantitative analysis of uranium and thorium and their separation. After the war, she returned to the Geological Survey and worked on chemistry of clay minerals and micas. She retired in 1965.

She died in 1970 at Silver Spring, Maryland.

83. Herman Francis Mark (1895 - 1992)

Herman Francis Mark was an Austrian-American chemist born in 1895 to Hermann Carl Mark and Lili Mueller. He worked for the development of polymer science using x-ray diffraction.

He worked at Polytechnic Institute of Brooklyn. In 1946, he established the Journal of Polymer Science.

He was involved in World War I as a part of Austro-Hungarian Army. Linus Pauling learned on X-ray diffraction from him. Albert Einstein asked Mark and his colleagues to work on verification of Compton Effect. He made serious attempts for the commercialization of polystyrene, polyvinyl chloride, polyvinyl alcohol and first synthetic rubbers.

He died in 1992 at USA.

84. Morris Selig Kharasch (1895 – 1957)

Morris Selig Kharasch was a Russian chemist born in 1895 at Ukraine. He worked on free radical addition reactions and polymerizations. He demonstrated anti-Markovnikov addition.

He migrated to USA at the age of 13. He received Ph.D degree from the University of Chicago in 1919. In 1920, he worked on organo-mercuric derivatives. He synthesized an anti-bacterial agent thimerosal and patented it in 1928.

During World War II, he worked for American Synthetic Rubber Research Program. Later, he concentrated more on Grignard reaction.

He died in 1957.

85. Artturi I Virtanen (1895 – 1973)

Artturi Ilmari Virtanen was a Finnish chemist born in 1895 at Helsinki to Kaarlo Virtanen and Serafina Isotalo. He married Lilja Moisio. He received the Nobel Prize in chemistry in 1845 for his work on agricultural and nutition chemistry. He invented AIV silage, which improved milk production. He also invented a method for the preservation of butter. This resulted in increase in butter export from Finland.

He studied at the University of Helsinki. He further studied physical chemistry, soil chemistry and microbiology at the University of Münster and the University of Stockholm. In 1923, he worked with Hans von Euler-Chelpin at Sweden.

He returned to Finland and became lecturer at the University of Helsinki in 1924. In 1931, he became professor of biochemistry at the Helsinki University of Technology and in 1939 at the University of Helsinki.

He died in 1973 at Helsinki.

86. William F Giauque (1895 – 1982)

William Francis Giauque was a Canadian born American chemist born in 1895 at Niagara Falls. He received the Nobel Prize in Chemistry in 1949 for his work on properties of matter at temperature close to absolute zero. He spent all time of his career at the University of California, Berkeley.

He worked for Hooker Electro-Chemical Company at Niagara Falls. He decided to become a chemical engineer. He then entered college of chemistry of the University of California, Berkeley. He received his doctoral degree in 1922. Under the influence of Gilbert Lewis, he started research. Because of his outstanding performance he got job as instructor of chemistry at Berkeley in 1922. He became full professor in 1934. He retired in 1962.

He died in 1982 at Berkeley.

87. Wallace H Carothers (1896 – 1937)

Wallace Hume Carothers was an American chemist born in 1896 at Burlington. He married Helen Sweetman in 1936. He invented nylon. He was a group leader of DuPont Experimental Station laboratory. He worked on neoprene as well.

He studied at Tarkio College. He studied masters at University of Illinois. He worked as an instructor at the University of South Dakota for a year. Later, he returned to University of Illinois for his doctoral study under Roger Adams. He received Ph.D degree in 1924. He worked as a research assistant during 1922 and 1923. After completing his doctoral degree, he worked as an instructor at the University of Illinois.

In 1926, he moved to Harvard University and became an instructor. After 1927, he moved to DuPont. He died in 1937 at Philadelphia.

88. Leonid Andrussow (1896 –1988)

Leonid Andrussow was a German chemical engineer born in 1896 at Riga to Woldemar Georg. He married Irmgard Von Bredow in 1926. He is known for the production of hydrogen cyanide from ammonia and methane. This reaction is called as Andrussow oxidation.

He was graduated from the University of Riga. He was involved in Russian revolution as White cavalry officer. Later, he moved to Berlin to study at the Friedrich Wilhelms University for Ph.D degree under Walther Nernst. It is known that he had some ideas on rocket propellants.

He died in 1988 at the age of 92 at Paris.

89. Robert S Mulliken (1896-1986)

Robert Sanderson Mulliken was an American physicist and chemist born in 1869 at Newburyport. He is well known for the development of molecular orbital theory. He received the Nobel Prize in chemistry in 1966. He won Priestley Medal in 1983.

He received Bachelor of Science degree in chemistry from Massachusetts Institute of Technology in 1917. He worked during World War I by making poison gases under James B Conant. In 1919, he started to study at the University of Chicago for Ph.D degree and received it in 1921 by working on separation of isotopes of mercury by evaporation.

He went to the Harvard University to study spectrographic technique. He was associated with Robert Oppenheimer, John Van Vleck, Harold Urey, John Slater and Niels Bohr. Between 1925 and 1927, he travelled across Europe. He worked at the New York University and the University of Chicago. He died in 1986 at Arlington.

90. Erich Hückel (1896 – 1980)

Erich Armand Arthur Joseph Hückel was a German chemist born in 1896 at Berlin. He is remembered for his contribution to Debye–Hückel theory of electrolytic solutions and Hückel method of approximate molecular orbital calculations.

He studied physics and mathematics at the University of Göttingen. After receiving doctoral degree, he worked as an assistant at Göttingen and at Zürich under Peter Debye. He with Debye developed Debye–Hückel theory in 1923. He spent in UK and Denmark and worked with Niels Bohr. Later, he joined Technische Hochschule in Stuttgart. In 1935, he moved to Marburg as a professor. He was a member of the International Academy of Quantum Molecular Science.

He died in 1980.

91. Nikolay N Semyonov (1896 – 1986)

Nikolay Nikolayevich Semyonov was a Russian chemist born in 1896 at Saratov. He received the Nobel Prize in Chemistry in 1856 for his work on the mechanism of chemical transformation.

He was graduated from the Petrograd University in 1917, where he worked under Abram Fyodorovich Ioffe. In 1918, he moved to Samara during Russian civil war. Later, he moved to Petrograd Physico-Technical Institute. He served as its vice-director as well. He discovered a way to measure the magnetic field of an atomic nucleus with Pyotr Kapitsa. He also studied kinetics of condensation and adsorption of vapors, ionization in gases. He became professor in 1928. He organized the Institute of Chemical Physics and became it's first director.

He died in 1986 at Moscow.

92. Joseph H Simons (1897 – 1984)

Joseph H. Simons was a US chemist born in 1897 at Chicago. He is famous for the production of fluorocarbons in mass scale.

He studied at the University of Illinois and University of California. He received doctoral degree in 1923. He became professor of chemical engineering at Pennsylvania State College (now Pennsylvania State University).

He passed fluorine gas through a carbon arc to create fluorocarbon. He published these results in 1938. In 1940, he was recruited to the Manhattan project for the enrichment of uranium. His fluorocarbons were inert enough to withstand the corrosive effects of uranium hexafluoride. In 1950, he moved to University of Florida. He retired in 1967.

He died in 1984 at Gainesville.

93. Tadeusz Reichstein (1897 – 1996)

Tadeusz Reichstein was a Polish-Swiss chemist born in 1897 at Włocławek. He won the Nobel Prize in Physiology or Medicine in 1950.

He did his school education at Jena and migrated to Basel at the age of eight. He studied under Hermann Staudinger at the Technical University of Karlsruhe. He developed the synthesis of vitamin C. In 1937, he moved to the University of Basle as professor of pharmaceutical chemistry.

He received the Nobel prize in 1950 for his work on hormones of adrenal cortex.

Later, he became interested in the phytochemistry.

He died in 1996 at the age of 99 at Basel.

94. Cyril N Hinshelwood (1897 – 1967)

Sir Cyril Norman Hinshelwood was a British chemist born in 1897 at London to Norman Macmillan Hinshelwood. He is a Nobel laureate.

He studied at Westminster City School and Balliol College, Oxford.

He worked during World War I in an explosive factory. He taught at Trinity College, Oxford from 1921 to 1937. He moved to the University of Oxford as professor in 1937. He served in many advisory councils. He worked on molecular kinetics. He studied explosive reaction of hydrogen and oxygen, and described the phenomenon of chain reaction. He observed chemical changes in bacterial cell, which laid foundation of antibiotics.

Adsorption of reactants on the catalyst surface is the rate determining step, which is known as Langmuir-Hinshelwood process. He died in 1967 at London.

95. Ronald G W Norrish (1897 – 1978)

Ronald George Wreyford Norrish was a British chemist born in 1897 at Cambridge. He received the Nobel Prize in Chemistry in 1967 for the development of flash photolysis.

He studied at The Perse School, Emmanuel College and Eric Rideal. He was a prisoner in World War I. He rejoined Emmanuel College in 1925 as a research fellow. Later, he joined University of Cambridge. He worked more on photochemistry. He was a Fellow of the Royal Society.

He died in 1978 at Cambridge.

96. Irène Joliot-Curie (1897 – 1956)

Irène Joliot-Curie was a French chemist and physicist born in 1897 as the elder daughter of Marie Curie and Pierre Curie. She married Frédéric Joliot-Curie. She was awarded the Nobel Prize in Chemistry in 1935 with her husband for their work on artificial radioactivity. She was a member of French Alternative Energies and Atomic Energy Commission. The Curie family has the most Nobel laureates to date. She was a member of the French government and became undersecretary for Scientific Research. Her daughters Hélène and Pierre were also renowned scientists.

She died in 1956 from acute leukemia since she was exposed to polonium and X-rays.

97. Georg Wittig (1897 – 1987)

Georg Wittig was a German chemist born in 1897 at Berlin. He is well known for Wittig reaction. He won the Nobel Prize in Chemistry in 1979.

He studied at the University of Tübingen. He studied Ph.D at the University of Marburg. He was a close friend of Karl Ziegler. He became professor at the TU Braunschweig in 1932. Later, he joined the University of Freiburg, where he laid foundations to carbanion chemistry. In 1944, he joined the University of Tübingen as head of chemistry department. He developed the Wittig reaction at Tübingen. In 1956, he joined the University of Heidelberg as head of the organic chemistry department. He worked at the University of Heidelberg even after his retirement in 1967 and published papers until 1980. He received many awards. He died in 1987 at Heidelberg.

98. Karl W Ziegler (1898 – 1973)

Karl Waldemar Ziegler was a German chemist born in 1898 at Helsa to Karl Ziegler and Luise Rall Ziegler. He won the Nobel Prize in Chemistry in 1963 along with Giulio Natta for their work on polymerization reactions. He also worked on free-radicals, cyclic compounds and organometallic compounds.

He studied at the University of Marburg. He was involed in World War I as a soldier. He received his doctoral degree in 1920. He lectured at the University of Marburg and the University of Frankfurt. He became a professor at the University of Heidelberg in 1926. In 1936, he became professor and director of the Chemical Institute at the University of Halle-Saale. He was a visiting lecturer at the University of Chicago. Between 1943 and 1969, he was the director of the Max Planck Institute for Coal Research. He established German chemical society in 1949. He served as its president for five years. He died in 1973 at Mülheim.

99. Huang Minlon (1898 – 1979)

Huang Minlon was a Chinese organic chemist and pharmaceutical scientist born in 1898 at Yangzhou. He was responsible for the establishment of modern pharmaceutical industries in China.

He was graduated from the Zhejiang Provincial College of Medicine in 1918. He received PhD degree from the University of Berlin in 1924. In 1925, he went back to China and became a professor at the Zhejiang Provincial College of Medicine. From 1934 to 1940,he worked in Germany and the UK. In 1940, he returned to China and joined Academia Sinica. He died in 1979.

100. Katharine B Blodgett (1898 – 1979)

Katharine Burr Blodgett was an American chemist and physicist born in 1898 at Schenectady to Katharine Buchanan and George Reddington Blodgett. She worked on surface chemistry. She invented invisible or nonreflective glasses during her work at General Electric. She was the first woman to receive Ph.D from the University of Cambridge.

She studied at New York City's Rayson School. She entered Bryn Mawr College on a scholarship. In 1917, Irving Langmuir bought her to University of Chicago, where she studied adsorption under Harvey B. Lemon. She worked under Langmuir as a research scientist. She studied under Sir Ernest Rutherford and became the first woman to receive doctoral degree from the Cambridge University. Later, she worked for General Electric.

She died in 1979 at Schenectady.

101. Robert Sidney Cahn (1899 – 1981)

Robert Sidney Cahn was a British chemist born in 1899 at Hampstead. He is well known for his contribution to the development of Cahn–Ingold–Prelog priority rules in stereochemistry. He proposed these rules with Christopher Kelk Ingold and Vladimir Prelog in 1956.

He was a fellow of the Royal Institute of Chemistry. He was the editor of the Journal of the Chemical Society between in 1949 and 1963. He remained as its director of publications and research until his retirement in 1965.

He died in 1981.

102. Charles Prévost (1899-1983)

Charles Prévost was a French chemist born in 1899 at Champlitte to Georges Prévost and Marie Zimmermann. He married Eléonore Fumée in in 1899.

He studied at the University of Paris. In 1923, he entered the aggregation in physical sciences and worked as an assistant at the École Navale. In 1928, he received his Ph.D degree. He worked as a lecturer in Nancy from 1929 to 1933. Later, he became professor of chemistry at Lille. In 1941, he transferred to maître de conferences for organic chemistry. In 1953, he was the chair of organic chemistry.

103. Paul Hermann Müller (1899 – 1965)

Paul Hermann Müller was a Swiss chemist born in 1899 at Olten. He received the Nobel Prize in Medicine in 1948 for the discovery of insecticidal properties of DDT. He used it to control malaria and yellow fever.

He received diploma in 1919 and entered Basel University in the same year, where hes studied chemistry and studied inorganic chemistry under Friedrich Fichter. In 1922, he studied organic chemistry with Hans Rupe and received Ph.D degree on '*The chemical and electrochemical oxidation of asymmetrical m-xylidene and its mono- and di-methyl derivatives*' in 1925. He worked for J. R. Geigy AG as a research chemist, where he worked on synthetic plant-derived dyes and natural tanning agents. Later, he worked on plant protection. In 1937, he patented synthetic methods for rhodanide and cyanate based compounds. He also produced Graminone, a seed disinfectant.

He died in 1965 at Basel.

104. John Butler (1899 – 1977)

John Alfred Valentine Butler was an English chemist born in 1899 at Winchcombe to Alfred and Mary Ann. He is known for his work on electrode kinetics (Butler–Volmer equation). He studied at the University of Birmingham. He worked as Assistant Lecturer at the University College of Swansea. In 1926, he was appointed as lecturer in the University of Edinburgh under Sir James Walker. In 1946, he was appointed to Courtauld Institute of Biochemistry under Charles Dodds. In 1949, he moved to Chester Beatty Research Institute.

He died in 1977.

105. Jean Frédéric Joliot-Curie (1900 – 1958)

Jean Frédéric Joliot-Curie was a French scientist born in 1900 at Paris. He received the Nobel Prize in Chemistry for the discovery of artificial radioactivity. He married Irène Joliot-Curie.

In 1925, he joined Radium Institute as Marie Curie's assistant. He received doctoral degree on electrochemistry of radio-elements. In 1937, he joined Collège de France as professor. In 1940, at the time of Nazi invasion, he managed to smuggle his working documents and materials to England.

He served as director of the French National Centre for Scientific Research in 1945. He became the first High Commissioner for atomic energy. He oversaw the construction of the first French atomic reactor in 1948. He and Irène visited Moscow on the occasion of two hundred and twentieth anniversary of the Russian Academy of Science. He was a member of the French Academy of Sciences, receipient of the Stalin Peace Prize. He served as the president of the World Council of Peace.

He died in 1958 at Paris.

106. Richard Johann Kuhn (1900 – 1967)

Richard Johann Kuhn was an Austrian-German chemist born in 1900 at Vienna. He won the Nobel Prize in Chemistry in 1938 for his work on carotenoids and vitamins. He married Daisy Hartmann in 1928.

He attended lectures at the University of Vienna. He studied chemistry at the University of Munich and received doctorl degree in 1922 for his work on enzymes. He continued his career at Munich, ETH Zurich and from 1929 at the University of Heidelberg.

He worked on organic chemistry and biochemistry. He became Principal of the Institute for Chemistry at the Kaiser Wilhelm Institute for Medical Research. He was a visiting scientist at the University of Pennsylvania.

He died in 1967 at Heidelberg.

107. Shirō Akabori (1900 – 1992)

Shirō Akabori was a Japanese chemist born in 1900. He is remembered for the Akabori amino-acid reactions.

He was trained as a pharmacist at Chiba medical school (now Chiba University). After graduation in 1921, he joined Momotani Juntenkan, a pharmaceutical company. He was hired as an assistant to Nishizawa Yūshichi. He received doctoral degree in 1931.

From 1932 to 1935 he visited abroad. After his return, he joined Osaka University as assistant professor. In 1953, he became professor at the University of Tokyo. He was the Ditector of the Protein-Institute at the Osaka University.

He died in 1992 at Shizuoka.

108. Vincent du Vigneaud (1901 – 1978)

Vincent du Vigneaud was an American chemist born in 1900 at Chicago. He received the Nobel Prize in Chemistry in 1955 for his work on biologically important sulphur compounds. He married Zella Zon Ford in 1924.

He studied at the University of Illinois at Urbana-Champaign. In 1924, he received MS and joined DuPont. He joined the University of Rochester for his doctoral studies. He graduated on 'The Sulfur of Insulin' in 1927. After his postdoctoral studies at Johns Hopkins University under John Jacob Abel, he travelled across Europe. After his return, he joined the University of Illinois as a professor. In 1932, he joined the George Washington University and the Cornell Medical College in 1938. After his retirement, he held a position at the Cornell University.

He died in 1978 at White Plains.

109. Werner Emmanuel Bachmann (1901 – 1951)

Werner Emmanuel Bachmann was an American chemist born in 1901 at Detroit.

He studied chemistry and chemical engineering at the Wayne State University and the University of Michigan. He received Ph. D. Degree under the guidance of Moses Gomberg. He spent rest of his time at the University of Michigan.

He worked on physical organic chemistry and organic synthesis. He was a pioneer in steroid synthesis. He is well known for the Gomberg-Bachmann reaction for the synthesis of diaryl compounds from aryl diazonium chlorides.He developed a new process for the manufacture of explosive cyclotrimethylenetrinitramine (RDX). He died in 1951.

110. Linus Carl Pauling (1901 – 1994)

Linus Carl Pauling was an American chemist, biochemist and chemical engineer born in 1901 at Portland. He was a receipient of the Nobel Prize in Chemistry in 1954. He published more than 1200 papers and books. He is considered as one of the 20 greatest scientists of all time. For his peace activism, he received the Nobel Peace Prize in 1962.

Pauling was one of the founders of quantum chemistry and molecular biology. Besides, he also worked on orbital hybridisation. He introduced the first accurate scale of electronegativities of the elements. Further, he worked on structures of biological molecules. This work inspired Watson and Crick to crack the structure of DNA.

He died in 1994 at Big Sur, California.

111. Henry Eyring (1901 – 1981)

Henry Eyring was a Mexican-born United States chemist born in 1901 at Colonia Juárez. He worked on the rate of chemical reactions and intermediates.

He studied mining, engineering, metallurgy and chemistry at the University of Arizona. He received Ph.D degree from the University of California, Berkeley on *"A Comparison of the Ionization by, and Stopping Power for, Alpha Particles of Elements and Compounds"*. He worked as an instructor at the Princeton University from 1931 to 1946. Later, he joined the University of Utah as dean of graduate school. The chemistry building of this university is name in his honor. He published more than 600 research articles and 10 books.

He died in 1981 at Salt Lake City, Utah.

112. Kurt Alder (1902 – 1958)

Kurt Alder was a German chemist born in 1902 at Königshütte. He studied at the University of Berlin and at the University of Kiel. He received doctoral degree in 1926 under the supervision of Otto Paul Hermann Diels.

He was appointed as reader at Kiel. In 1936, he joined I G Farben Industrie, where he worked on synthetic rubber. In 1940, he was appointed as professor at the University of Cologne. He was the director of the Institute of Chemistry there. He worked on synthesis of organic compounds and published more than 151 articles. He received the Nobel Prize in chemistry along with Otto Paul Hermann Diels for the invention of Diels–Alder reaction.

He died in 1958 at Cologne.

113. Arne Tiselius (1902 – 1971)

Arne Wilhelm Kaurin Tiselius was a Swedish scientist born in 1902 at Stockholm. He received the Nobel Prize in Chemistry in 1948 for his work on electrophoresis and adsorption analysis and discovery of complex nature of the serum proteins.

He studied at the Uppsala University and received his Ph.D degree in 1930. He published many articles on diffusion and adsorption in naturally occurring base-exchanging zeolites. He visited the Princeton University. He returned to the Uppsala University and continued to work on proteins.

He died in 1971 at Uppsala.

114. Lars Onsager (1903 – 1976)

Lars Onsager was a Norwegian-born American chemist and physicist. He received the Nobel Prize in Chemistry in 1968.

He studied chemical engineering at the Norwegian Institute of Technology. He proposed a correction to the Debye-Hückel theory of electrolytic solutions. He convinced Debye that his theory was wrong. He was invited by Debye to work as his assistant at the Eidgenössische Technische Hochschule.

In 1928, he joined the Johns Hopkins University. Later, he joined the Brown University, where he contributed to statistical mechanics and thermodynamics. Then he joined the Yale University.

He died in 1976 at Coral Gables.

115. Giulio Natta (1903 – 1979)

Giulio Natta was an Italian chemist born in 1903 at Imperia. He won the Nobel Prize in Chemistry in 1963 with Karl Ziegler for their work on polymers.

He received chemical engineering degree from Politecnico di Milano in 1924. In 1927, he became professor. In 1933, he became professor at the Pavia University. In 1935, he shifted to the University of Rome. Between 1936 and 1938, he was a full professor and director of the Institute of Industrial Chemistry at the Polytechnic Institute of Turin. In 1938, he was the head of the department of chemical engineering at the Politecnico di Milano University. He was a recipient of of Lomonosov Gold Medal in 1969. He died in 1979 at Bergamo, Italy.

116. Adolf Butenandt (1903 – 1995)

Adolf Friedrich Johann Butenandt was a German biochemist born in 1903 at Bremerhaven. He was a recipient of the Nobel Prize in Chemistry in 1939 for his work on sex harmones. Initially, he rejected the award due to government policy, but accepted in 1949 after World War II.

He studied at the University of Marburg. He joined the University of Göttingen to persue doctoral degree. He became a professor at the Technical University of Danzig. He was the President of the Max Planck Society between 1960 and 1972. He discovered the sex pheromone of silkworms, which he named as bombykol.

He died in 1995 at Munich.

117. Charles John Pedersen (1904 – 1989)

Charles John Pedersen was an American chemist born in Busan, Korea to Brede Pedersen and Takino Yasui. He is well known for the synthesis of crown ethers. He worked as a chemist for Dupont. He shared the Nobel Prize in Chemistry in 1987 with Donald J. Cram and Jean-Marie Lehn.

He completed his primary education in Japan. He studied chemical engineering at the University of Dayton, USA. Later, he decided to build his career without any support from his father. He is one of the few people who won the Nobel Prize in sicence without a Ph.D degree. Later, he studied at the Massachusetts Institute of Technology. After leaving this institution, he joined DuPont Company.

He died in 1989 at Salem, USA.

118. Wendell M Stanley (1904 – 1971)

Wendell Meredith Stanley was an American chemist born in 1904 at Indiana. He was married to Marian Staples in 1929.

He studied B.Sc. at Earlham College and Ph.D at University of Illinois. He has written a chemistry book 'Chemistry: A beautiful thing'.

He visited Munich and returned to USA in 1931. He started work at the Rockfeller Institute for Medical Research. In 1948, he joined the University of California as a professor. He worked on lepracidal compounds, stereochemistry of biphenyls and chemistry of sterols. Further, he worked on virus, which causes mosaic disease in tobacco. He was awarded the chemistry Nobel Prize in 1946.

He died in 1971.

119. Carolina H MacGillavry (1904 – 1993)

Carolina Henriette MacGillavry was a Dutch chemist and crystallographer born in 1904 at Amsterdam. She worked on diffraction in crystallography.

She studied chemistry at the University of Amsterdam. In 1937, she received her doctoral degree. She became an assistant to A. E. van Arkel. She worked with Bijvoet on crystallography. She developed direct methods in which calculus can be used in crystallography. She worked with Pepinsky in Alabama in 1948.

In 1950, she was appointed to the Royal Netherlands Academy of Arts and Sciences. She was appointed as professor to the University of Amsterdam and retired in 1972.

She died in 1993 at Amsterdam.

120. Daulat Singh Kothari (1906 – 1993)

Daulat Singh Kothari was an Indian chemist born in 1906 to Jain at Rajasthan. He received early education at Udaipur and Indore. He was post graduated from the Allahabad University under the supervision of Meghnad Saha. He was awarded the Ph.D degree from the University of Cambridge under the guidance of Ernest Rutherford.

After his return from UK, he joined the Delhi University. He served as scientific advisor to Ministry of Defence, chairman of the University Grants Commission. He received Padma Bushan and Padma Vibhushan award from the Government of India. He was responsible for the establishment of many labs in India. He was the president of the Indian Science Congress in 1963.

He died in 1993 at Delhi.

121. Vladimir Prelog (1906 – 1998)

Vladimir Prelog was a Croatian-Swiss organic chemist born in 1906. He received the Nobel Prize in Chemistry for his work on stereochemistry.

He completed school education in Sarajevo and Zagreb. He studied diploma in chemical engineering in the Czech Technical University.

He started his career by joining to the University of Zagreb as lecturer in 1935, where he worked on organic chemistry and chemical engineering.

He died in 1998 at Zurich, Switzerland.

122. Max Tishler (1906 – 1989)

Max Tishler was an American chemist born in 1906 at Boston. He is well known for the synthesis of ascorbic acid, riboflavin, pyridoxine, nicotinamide, threonine and tryptophan. Also, he is popular for the development of fermentation processes for actinomycin, vitamin B12, streptomycin and penicillin. He invented sulfaquinoxaline to treat coccidiosis.

He studied bachelor's degree at Tufts College and Ph.D in organic chemistry at Harvard University. Later, he worked at Merck. After his retirement he taught chemistry at Wesleyan University.

He died in 1989 at Middletown.

123. Hazel Gladys Bishop (1906 – 1998)

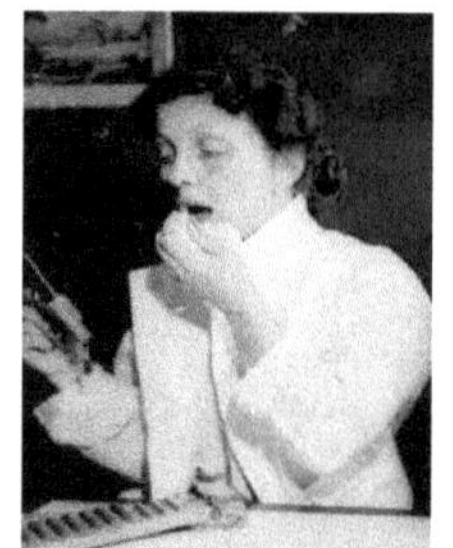

Hazel Gladys Bishop was an American chemist born in 1906 at Hoboken. She was the founder of cosmetics company Hazel Bishop Inc. She is well known for the invention of the first long-lasting lipstick.

She studied at Barnard College in New York. Betwween 1935 and 1942, she worked at Columbia University College of physicians and surgeons. In 1942, she worked for Standard Oil Development Company as a chemist for designing fuels for airplanes during World War II. In 1945, she joined Socony Vacuum Oil Company.

She was involved in many professional organizations. She was widely recognized by the American Institute of Chemists. She was actively engaged in American Chemical Society and the Society of Women Engineers.

She died in 1998 at Rye, New York.

124. Luis Federico Leloir (1906 – 1987)

Luis Federico Leloir was an Argentine physician and biochemist born in 1906 at Paris, France to Federico Augusto Rufino Leloir Bernal and Hortensia Aguirre de Leloir. He received the 1970 Nobel Prize in Chemistry for the discovery of the metabolic pathways in lactose.

He studied at the University of Buenos Aires. His work on nucleotides, carbohydrate metabolism and renal hypertension gave him international recognition.

He died in 1987 at Argentina.

125. Alexander R Todd (1907 – 1997)

Alexander Robertus Todd was a Scottish biochemist born in 1907 at Cathcart to Alexander Todd and Jane Lowry. He received the Nobel Prize in chemistry in 1957 for his work on synthesis of nucleotides, nucleosides and nucleotide coenzymes.

He studied B.Sc. at the University of Glasgow. He received Ph.D degree from the Johann Wolfgang Goethe University of Frankfurt am Main in 1931 by working on chemistry of bile acids. He was awarded a research fellowship from the Royal Commission for the Exhibition of 1951. He received another doctoral degree in 1933.

He worked at the Lister Institute, the University of Edinburgh and the University of London. He was a visiting professor at California Institute of Technology. He was the director of chemical laboratories at the University of Manchester. He was honoured as Fellow of the Royal Society and the President of the Royal Society. He died in 1997 at Oakington.

126. Edwin Mattison McMillan (1907 – 1991)

Edwin Mattison McMillan was an American scientist born in 1907 at California. He discovered an element Neptunium. For this discovery, he shared the Nobel Prize in Chemistry in 1951 with Glenn Seaborg.

He was graduated from the California Institute of Technology. He earned Ph.D degree from the Princeton University in 1933. He joined the Berkeley Radiation Loboratory, where he discovered oxygen-15 and beryllium-10. He worked on microwave radar at the MIT Radiation Laboratory during World War II. At the same time he worked on sonar at the Navy Radio and Sound Laboratory. In 1942, he joined the Manhattan Project. He co-invented the synchrotron with Vladimir Veksler. After World War II, he returned to the Berkeley Radiation Laboratory and worked there until his retirement.

He died in 1991 at California.

127. Mary Elliott Hill (1907–1969)

Mary Elliott Hill was an African-American chemist born in 1907 at South Mills, North Carolina to Robert Elliott and Frances Bass. She worked on organic chemistry and analytical chemistry. She studied the properties of ultraviolet light and synthesis of ketenes. She was the first African-American women, who received the master's degree in chemistry.

She studied at Virginia State College for Negroes and University of Pennsylvania. She worked at Bennett College and Tennessee A and I State College.

She died in 1969 at Frankfort, US.

128. Edward Teller (1908-2003)

Edward Teller was a Hungarian-American scientist born in 1908 at Budapest. He is popularly called as the father of the hydrogen bomb. He contributed to nuclear and molecular physics, spectroscopy, surface physics, Thomas-Fermi theory, density functional theory, quantum mechanical treatment of complex molecules. He worked in Manhattan Project. He was a co-founder of Lawrence Livermore National Laboratory.

He was supported by US government for military research establishment. He received many awards like Enrico Fermi Award and Albert Einstein Award.

He died in 2003 at Stanford, California.

129. Willard Frank Libby (1908 – 1980)

Willard Frank Libby was an American chemist born in 1908 at Grand Valley, Colorado. He developed radiocarbon dating, which is a process used in archaeology and palaeontology. For this contribution, he received the Nobel Prize in Chemistry in 1960.

He received doctoral degree from the University of California, Berkeley. He studied radioactive elements. He developed sensitive Geiger counters to measure weak and artificial radioactivity. He worked in Manhattan Project during World War II by developing gaseous diffusion process for uranium enrichment.

After the World War II, he joined the Institute for Nuclear Studies of University of Chicago as professor. Here, he developed C^{14} dating of organic compounds.

He died in 1980 at Los Angeles.

130. Myrtle Claire Bachelder (1908 – 1997)

Myrtle Claire Bachelder was an American chemist born in 1908 at Worcester, Massachusetts. She worked as Women's Army Corps officer in Manhattan Project.

She studied bachelor's degree at Middlebury College and master of education degree at Boston University.

In Manhattan Project, she did analysis of the spectroscopy of uranium isotopes. Besides, she worked on uranium enrichment.

She died in 1997 at Chicago.

131. Melvin Spencer Newman (1908 – 1993)

Melvin Spencer Newman was an Americaan chemist born in 1908 at New York city. He was a professor at Ohio State University. He is well known for developing Newman projection formula.

He studied at Riverdale Country School and Yale University. He received Ph.D degree in 1932 under the guidance of Professor Rudolph J. Anderson. He did postdoctoral studies at Columbia University and Harvard University. Later, he started independent career at Ohio State University.

He was a member of Phi Lanbda Upsilon, Sigma Xi, Alpha Epsilon Delta, American Association for the Advancement of Science and American Chemical Society. He was elected as a member to National Academy of Sciences in 1956.

He received many awards namely American Chemical Society Award, Morley Medal, Wilbur Lucius Cross Medal, honorary doctorate from University of New Orleans and Joseph Sullivant medal. He died in 1993.

132. Arthur C Cope (1909-1966)

Arthur C Cope was an American chemist born in 1909 at Dunreith, Indiana. He is well known for the invention of Cope elimination and Cope rearrangement.

He studied at the Butler University. He received Ph.D degree from the University of Wisconsin-Madison in 1932. He continued research at the Harvard University in 1933 as a National Research Council Fellow. Later, he joined Bryn Mawr College. In 1941, he moved to Columbia University and in 1945 to Massachusetts Institute of Technology. He was a member of National Academy of Sciences.

He died in 1966 at Washington DC.

133. Archer Martin (1910 – 2002)

Archer John Porter Martin was a British chemist born in 1910 at London. He won 1952 Nobel Prize in Chemistry with Richard Synge for the invention of partition chromatography.

He worked at Dunn Nutritional Laboratory, Wool Industries Research Institution, Medical Research Council and National Institute for Medical Research.

He developed partition chromatography, for which he received the Nobel Prize.

Later, he developed gas-liquid chromatography.

He was a visiting professor at the University of Houston. He published around 70 articles.

He died in 2002 at Llangarron.

134. Dorothy Hodgkin (1910 – 1994)

Dorothy Mary Crowfoot Hodgkin was a British chemist born in 1910 at Cairo. She received the Nobel Prize in Chemistry for her work on development of X-ray crystallography to determine the structure of biomolecules. She established the structure of penicillin, vitamin B_{12} and insulin.

She studied chemistry at Somerville College, Oxford. She worked for Ph.D degree at Newnham College, Cambridge. During her doctoral studies, she got knowledge of X-ray crystallography. She determined the structure of proteins like pepsin. She was awarded with a Ph.D degree in 1937 for her work on X-ray crystallography and the chemistry of sterols.

She died in 1994 at Ilmington.

135. Paul John Flory (1910 – 1985)

Paul John Flory was an American chemist born in 1910 at Sterling. Illinois. He received 1974 Nobel Prize in Chemistry for his work on polymers and macromolecules.

He studied B.Sc. degree at Manchester College (Indiana) and Ph.D at the Ohio State University. He worked at DuPont.

He received Charles Goodyear Medal, Priestley Medal and the American Academy of Achievement award.

He died in 1985 at Big Sur.

136. Jacques Lucien Monod (1910 – 1976)

Jacques Lucien Monod was a French biochemist born in 1910 at Paris. He received the Nobel Prize in Physiology or Medicine in 1965 for his work on genetic control of enzyme and virus synthesis.

He worked at the California Institute of Technology on Drosophila genetics.

He died in 1976 at France.

137. Melvin Ellis Calvin (1911 – 1997)

Melvin Ellis Calvin was an American biochemist born in 1911 at Minnesota to Elias Calvin and Rose Herwitz. He married Marie Genevieve Jemtegaard in 1942. He discovered the Calvin cycle along with Andrew Benson and James Bassham. For this work, he was awarded the Nobel Prize in Chemistry in 1961.

He studied B.Sc. at the Michigan College of Mining and Technology in 1931. He worked for doctoral degree at the University of Minnesota. Later, he was a postdoctoral fellow at the University of Manchester.

He joined the University of California, Berkeley in 1937. He became professor in 1947. He traced the complete route that carbon travels during photosynthesis.

In 1963, he got additional title of Professor of Molecular Biology. He was the founder and director of the Laboratory of Chemical Biodynamics. At the same time, he was the associate director of Berkeley Radiation Laboratory.

He died in 1997 at Berkeley.

138. William Howard Stein (1911 – 1980)

William Howard Stein was an American chemist born in 1911 at New York City to Fred M. Stein and Beatrice Borg Stein. He determined ribonuclease sequence. For this work he received the Nobel Prize in Chemistry in 1972. He invented automatic amino acid analyzer. He contributed to the advancement of chromatography such as liquid chromatography and gas chromatography.

He did his post graduation at Harvard University in 1929 and he was graduated from Columbia University in 1936. In 1937, he completed his thesis.

He was a professor at Rockefeller Institute. He served as a visiting scientist at the University of Chicago and the Harvard University.

He died in 1980 at New York City.

139. Ewart Jones (1911 – 2002)

Sir Ewart Ray Herbert Jones was a Welsh chemist born in 1911 at Wrexham. He worked on natural products like steroids, terpenes and vitamins. He developed the Jones oxidation.

He studied at the University College of North Wales, Bangor. Here he married Frances Copp. He started his career as lecturer at Imperial College of Science and Technology. Later, he joined the University of Manchester.

He died in 2002.

140. Glenn Theodore Seaborg (1912 – 1999)

Glenn Theodore Seaborg was an American chemist born in 1912 at Michigan. He worked on synthesis, discovery and investigation of transuranium elements. For this contribution, he received the 1951 Nobel Prize in Chemistry. His research leads to the development of actinide series in the periodic table of the elements.

He worked at the University of California, Berkeley. He contributed to the commercial use of nuclear energy for peaceful work.

He contributed for the discovery of plutonium, curium, americium, berkelium, californium, einsteinium, mendelevium, fermium and nobelium. An element with atomic number 106 was named in his honor as seaborgium. Also, he discovered more than 100 isotopes of transuranium elements. He postulated the existence of super-heavy elements (transactinide and superactinide series).

He died in 1999 at California.

141. Herbert Charles Brown (1912 – 2004)

Herbert Charles Brown was an American chemist born in 1912 at London. He recieved the Nobel Prize in Chemistry in 1979 for his work on organoboranes.

He studied at the University of Chicago for his Ph. D degree. He served as an instructor at the same university. Later, he joined Wayne University as assistant professor. Further, he moved to Purdue University as professor.

He received the National Medal of Science.

He died in 2004 at Indiana.

142. Stanford Moore (1913 – 1982)

Stanford Moore was an American chemist born in 1913 at Chicago. He received the 1972 Nobel Prize in Chemistry for his work on ribonuclease along with Christian B Anfinsen and William Howard Stein.

He studied at the Vanderbilt University. He received Ph.D degree from the University of Wisconsin-Madison in 1938. Later, he served at the Rockefeller University. In 1952, he became professor of biochemistry. In 1958, he and William H Stein jointly developed the first automated amino acid analyzer, which helped the determination of protein sequences.

He died in 1982 at New York.

143. Richard Synge (1914 – 1994)

Richard Laurence Millington Synge was a British chemist born in 1914 at Liverpool. He won the Nobel Prize in Chemistry in 1952 for the invention of partition chromatography along with Archer Martin.

He studied at Winchester College and Trinity College. He worked at the Wool Industries Research Association, Lister Institute for Preventive Medicine, Rowett Research Institute and Food Research Institute.

He developed partition chromatography and he studied peptides of gramicidin.

In 1950, he was elected as a Fellow of the Royal Society.

He died in 1994 at Norwich.

144. Max F Perutz (1914 – 2002)

Max Ferdinand Perutz was a Austrian-born British chemist born in 1914 at Vienna. He received the Nobel Prize for Chemistry for his work on haemoglobin and myoglobin.

He studied his undergraduate degree at the University of Vienna. He worked for his doctoral degree under the supervision of Lawrence Bragg.

He was awarded with the Medal of the Royal Society in 1971. Also, he received the Copley Medal in 1979.

He was elected to the Royal Society as a fellow in 1954.

He died in 2002 at Cambridge.

145. Arthur John Birch (1915 – 1995)

Arthur John Birch was an Australian chemist born in 1915 at Sydney. He is well known for the invention of the Birch reduction, which is most commonly used in organic chemistry. In 1948, he published the first total synthesis of 19-nortestosterone, which is a male sex hormone. He also contributed for the synthesis of many steroid drugs and antibiotics. He also developed the synthesis ring A-B of cholesterol. He published around 440 research articles and reports.

He studied at the University of Sydney and at the University of Oxford. He worked with Sir Robert Robinson. He served as a professor at the University of Sydney, he was appointed as a fellow of the Australian Academy of Science in 1954. He became a fellow of the Rotal society in 1958. Besides, he served as President of the Australian Academy of Science.

He died in 1995 at Canberra.

146. Jeanne Beadle Burbank (1915 – 2002)

Jeanne Beadle Burbank was an American chemist born in 1915 at Philadelphia to John Bookwalter Beadle. She worked at United States Naval Research Laboratory on lead-acid and silver-zinc batteries used in submarines.

She studied at the American University in Washington, D. C. She married Robert Clowe Burbank in 1936. The couple worked at a laboratory in Philadelphia. They studied colloidal chemistry at the University of Pennsylvania. Her husband died of Hodgkin's lymphoma in 1946. Later, she returned to Washington, D.C. and joined United States Naval Research Laboratory. In 1971, she retired.

She died in 2002 at Phoenix.

147. Henry Taube (1915 – 2005)

Henry Taube was a Canadian-born American chemist born in 1915 at Neudorf. He was awarded the Nobel Prize in Chemistry in 1983 for his work on mechanisms of electron-transfer reactions in metal complexes. He was the second Canadian-born chemist, who won the Nobel Prize.

He studied at the University of Saskatchewan for his undergraduate and postgraduate degree. He worked for doctoral degree at the University of California, Berkeley. He worked at the Cornell University, the University of Chigaco and Stanford University. He received the Priestley Medal and many honorary doctorates. He published around 600 research articles and mentored over 200 students in his career.

He died in 2005 at Palo Alto, California.

148. Jan Boldingh (1915 – 2003)

Jan Boldingh was a Dutch chemist born in 1915 at Buitenzorg.

He studied and worked at the Utrecht University. He discovered new analytical techniques such as gas chromatography, coupling of gas chromatography with mass spectrometry. He was interested in the study of role of fats in nutrition.

He was a member of the Royal Netherlands Academy of Arts and Sciences.

He died in 2003 at Schiedam.

149. Arthur Donald Walsh (1916 – 1977)

Arthur Donald Walsh was a British chemist born in 1916 to Arthur Thomas Walsh. He worked as a professor of chemistry at the University of Dundee. He is well known for the discovery of Walsh diagrams and Walsh rules in inorganic chemistry.

He received Mawson scholarship in 1938 to study at the Corpus Christi College, Cambridge. He worked with W C Price on spectra of triple- and double-bonded molecules. He got PhD degree in 1941. Prof. R G W Norrish invited him to work on knock in combustion engines. He continued work at Cambridge on both spectroscopy and combustion. He joined the University of Leeds as a lecturer. He was a visiting professor at the University of California. Later, he joined Queen's College, Dundee and then to the University of St Andrews.

He was a fellow of the Royal Society of Edinburgh and the Royal Society.

He died in 1977.

150. Christian B Anfinsen Jr. (1916 – 1995)

Christian Boehmer Anfinsen Jr. was an American chemist born in 1916 at Monessen, Pennsylvania to Sophie and Christian Boehmer Anfinsen Sr. He won the Nobel Prize in Chemistry in 1972 for his work on ribonuclease and amino acid sequence analysis.

He studied B. Sc. in chemistry at Swarthmore College. He received master's degree from the University of Pennsylvania. He moved to Carlsberg laboratory at Denmark to study methods of analysis and chemical structure of bulky proteins such as enzymes under American-Scandinavian fellowship. Later, he joined Harvard Medical School to pursue his doctoral degree. In 1950, he was appointed as chief to the National Heart Institute, Maryland. In 1954, he revisited the Carlsberg laboratory under Rockefeller foundation fellowship. Between 1958 and 1959, he spent time at the Weizmann Institute of Science, Israel. In 1962, he moved to Harvard Medical School as a visiting professor. Later, he was appointed to the National Institute of Arthritis and Metabolic Diseases as the chief of laboratory of chemical biology. He spent his rest of the time by working at Johns Hopkins.

He died in 1995 at Randallstown, Maryland.

151. Ronald Sydney Nyholm (1917 – 1971)

Ronald Sydney Nyholm was an Australian chemist born in 1917 at Broken Hill, New South Wales to Eric Edward Nyholm. He studied at the University of Sydney and the University College London. He worked in Eveready Battery Co for sometime. He joined the Sydney Technical College as lecturer. Later, he was an associate professor at the New South Wales University of Technology. Finally, he was migrated to the University College London as professor.

He died in 1971 at Cambridge, London.

152. William S Knowles (1917-2012)

William Standish Knowles was an American chemist born in Taunton, Massachusetts. He received the Nobel Prize in chemistry in 2001 for his work on hydrogenation reactions in asymmetric synthesis along with Ryoji Noyori.

He studied at the Columbia University.

He died in 2012 at Chesterfield, Missouri, United States.

153. Robert B Woodward (1917 – 1979)

Robert Burns Woodward was an American chemist born in 1917 at Boston. He worked on total synthesis of complex natural products and their structural elucidation. He also worked with Roald Hoffmann on theoretical studies of chemical reactions. For these works, he was awarded the 1965 Nobel Prize in Chemistry.

He received the Bachelor's degree and the doctoral degree from the Massachusetts Institute of Technology. He worked on the synthesis of estrone, which is a female sex hormone. He was a postdoctoral fellow at the University of Illinois. Later, he received a fellowship to work at Harvard University and remained there at various capacities. Further, he was awarded the Donner Professor of Science, which freed him from regular teaching jobs and he could devote his whole time to research. In 1940s, he designed rules for absorption of compounds in UV spectroscopy, which are popularly known as Woodward's rules. In 1944, he reported the total synthesis of alkaloid quinine, which is used to treat malaria. During 1940s, he synthesized cholesterol, strychnine, cortisone, lysergic acid, chlorophyll, reserpine, cephalosporin and colchicines. He died in 1979 at Cambridge, Massachusetts.

154. John Cornforth Jr. (1917 – 2013)

Sir John Warcup Cornforth Jr. Was an Australian-British chemist born in 1917 at Sydney to John Warcup Cornforth and Hilda Eipper. He married Rita Harradence. He received the Nobel Prize in Chemistry in 1975 for his work on the stereochemistry of enzymes catalyzed reactions.

He was educated at Sydney Boy's High School and the University of Sydney. He studied organic chemistry in his bachelor's degree. He was partially deaf in those days. They both got fellowships to visit UK. At the University of Oxford, he was at St. Catherine's College and his wife was at Somerville College. During their stay in UK they collaborated with Sir Robert Robinson. He worked on the chemistry of penicillin, sterol and cholesterol. He was able to synthesize non-aromatic steroid with Robert Burns Woodward. Later, he joined the University of Warwick as professor and then migrated to the University of Sussex.

He died in 2013 at Sussex.

155. Ilya R Prigogine (1917 – 2003)

Ilya Romanovich Prigogine was a Russian chemist born in 1917 at Moscow. He received the Nobel Prize in Chemistry for his work on dissipative structures, complex systems and irreversibility.

His family left Russia in 1921 and migrated to Germany. Next, they moved to Belgium in 1929, where he got Belgian nationality in 1949. He studied at the Free University of Brussels and became professor of the same university. Later, he worked at the University of Texas at Austin. He was a visiting professor at Northwestern University.

He died in 2003 at Brussels.

156. Herbert A Hauptman (1917 – 2011)

Herbert Aaron Hauptman was an American Scientist born in 1917 at New York City to Leah and Israel Hauptman. He married Edith Citrynell in 1940. He received 1985 Nobel Prize in Chemistry for his work on development of methods to solve the structures of crystalline compounds.

He studied mathematics at the Columbia University and Ph.D in physics at the University of Maryland. His broad knowledge in both these areas led him to solve problems in X-ray crystallography. Later, he also received Ph.D. in mathematics

He has published more than 170 research articles. He was the director and president of Medical Foundation of Buffalo.

He died in 2011 at Buffalo, New York.

157. John Bennett Fenn (1917 - 2010)

John Bennett Fenn was an American chemist born in 1917 at New York City. He was the recipient of 2002 Nobel Prize in Chemistry for his work on electrospray ionization in mass spectrometry.

He studied bachelor's degree at Berea College and Ph.D at Yale Univeersity.

He joined Yale and Virginia Commonwealth University after working at industries based at Monsanto.

He has published over 100 research articles including a book.

He died in 2010 at Richmond, Virginia.

158. Ernst Otto Fischer (1918 – 2007)

Ernst Otto Fischer was a German chemist born in 1918 at Munich to Karl T. Fischer and Valentine née Danzer. He received the Nobel Prize in chemistry for his work on organometallic chemistry.

He studied at the Technical University of Munich. He worked for Ph.D degree on 'The mechanisms of carbon monoxide reactions of nickel(II) salts in the presence of dithionites and sulfoxylates' under the guidance of Walter Hieber. He proposed the structure of ferrocene and established structures of nicklocene, cabaltocene and bis(benzene)chromium. He was a member of Bavarian Academy of Sciences and German Academy of Natural Scientists, Leopoldina. He has published around 450 research articles. He was a visiting professor at many universities.

He died in 2007 at Munich.

159. Frederick Sanger (1918 – 2013)

Frederick Sanger was an English chemist born in 1918 at Rendcomb, England to Frederick Sanger and Cicely Sanger. He won the Nobel Prize in Chemistry twice. Once for determination of amino acid sequence of insulin and other proteins. Another for determining DNA sequenceing technique.

He studied at St John's College, Cambridge. He worked for Ph.D degree under the guidance of N.W. Bill Pirie on 'The metabolism of the amino acid lysine in the animal body'.

He is one of the few people who received multiple Nobel Prizes in the same category and one of five persons with two Nobel Prizes.

He died in 2013 at Cambridge.

160. Kenichi Fukui (1918 – 1998)

Kenichi Fukui was a Japanese chemist born in 1918 at Ikoma district to Ryokichi Fukui. He was the first East Asian who received the Nobel Prize in Chemistry. He worked on determination of mechanisms of chemical reactions. He explained the role of frontier orbitals in chemical reactions.

He studied at the Kyoto University. He worked in theoretical and experimental chemistry. He was graduated from the Kyoto Imperial University in 1941. He joined Army Fuel Laboratory of Japan at the time of World War II. He took lecturer position at Kyoto Imperial University in 1943.

Later, he joined the Kyoto University as a professor of physical chemistry. He served as a president of Kyoto Institute of Technology, member of the International Academy of Quantum Molecular Science. He was the director of the Institute for Fundamental Chemistry from 1988 till his death.

He died in 1998 at Kyoto.

161. Jacob Akiba Marinsky (1918 – 2005)

Jacob Akiba Marinsky was an American chemist born in 1918 at Buffalo, New York. He was the co-discoverer of the element promethium.

He studied at the State University of New York and received bachelor's degree in 1939. He worked as a chemist for the Manhattan Project. Later, he received doctoral degree from the Massachusetts Institute of Technology on nuclear chemistry in 1949.

He died in 2005 at the age of 87.

162. Derek Barton (1918 – 1998)

Sir Derek Harold Richard Barton was an English chemist born in 1918 at Gravesend, Kent to William Thomas and Maude Henrietta Barton. He was a recipient of the Nobel Prize in Chemistry in 1969.

He studied at Imperial College London for graduation and Ph.D. in organic chemistry. Later, he started working at Imperial College. He was a visiting lecturer at the Harvard University. Then, he was promoted as reader and then as professor at Birkbeck college. In 1955, he joined the University of Glasgow and in 1957 he joined the University of Oxford. His work on development of the concept of conformation and its application in chemistry won him the Nobel Prize. He was a visiting professor to the Massachusetts Institute of Technology and the University of Illinois. He was a member of the American Academy of Arts and Sciences. He received many medals and prizes.

He died in 1998 at Texas, USA at the age of 79.

163. Jens Christian Skou (1918 – 2018)

Jens Christian Skou was a Danish chemist born in 1918 at Lemvig to Magnus Martinus Skou and Ane-Margrethe Skou.

He was graduated from the University of Copenhagen in medicine in 1944 and received Ph.D degree in 1954. He started work at Aarhus University and became professor in 1977. He retired in 1988.

He received the Nobel Prize in Chemistry in 1997 for the discovery of Na^+, K^+-ATPase. He explained the theory of anaesthesia.

He died in 2018 at the age of 99.

164. Paul Delos Boyer (1918 – 2018)

Paul Delos Boyer was an American chemist born in 1918 at Provo. He was a professor at University of California, Los Angeles. He won the 1997 Nobel Prize in Chemistry for his work on biosynthesis of adenosine triphosphate (ATP).

He studied chemistry at Brigham Young University and obtained doctoral degree from the University of Wisconsin–Madison in 1943. He worked at the Stanford University for several years. He started independent research at the University of Minnesota. He developed kinetic, isotopic and chemical methods to investigate enzyme mechanisms. In 1963, he joined the University of California, Los Angeles as professor. In 1965, he was the founding director of the Molecular Biology Institute. He was the editor of the Annual Review of Biochemistry from 1963 to 1989.

He died in 2018 at the age of 99.

165. Lawrence E Glendenin (1918 – 2008)

Lawrence Elgin Glendenin was an American chemist born in 1918 at Bay City. He was the co-discoverer of the element promethium.

He studied at the University of Chicago. He worked in Clinton Laboratories during World War II on separation, identification and characterization of radioactive elements produced by nuclear fission. In 1945, together with Jacob A Marinsky and Charles D Coryell, he discovered promethium. They extracted it from fission products. Also, they produced it by bombarding neodymium with neutrons and isolated it by means of ion-exchange chromatography. Publication of its discovery was delayed due to World War II. In 1947, Marinsky and Glendenin disclosed this discovery in an American Chemical Society meeting.

He died in 2008 at the age of 90 at Illinois.

166. Ralph G Pearson (1919-2022)

Ralph Gottfrid Pearson was an American chemist born in 1919 at Chicago. He is well known for developing the concept 'hard and soft acids and bases'.

He received doctoral degree from the Northwestern University in 1943. He worked in the same university from 1946 to 1976. Later, he moved to the University of California at Santa Barbara and worked there until his death. He worked on ligand field theory, physical organic chemistry and coordination chemistry.

He proposed a theory of hard and soft acids and bases (HSAB) in 1963. With Robert Parr, in 1983 he redefined HSAB theory into a quantitative method by calculating absolute hardness by utilizing density functional theory. He died in 2022 at the age of 103.

167. William N Lipscomb Jr. (1919 – 2011)

William Nunn Lipscomb Jr. was an American chemist born in 1919 at Cleveland, Ohio. He worked on boron chemistry, theoretical chemistry, biochemistry nuclear magnetic resonance and chemical shift.

He received Bachelor's degree from the University of Kentucky in 1941 and the doctoral degree from the California Institute of Technology n 1946. Later, he worked at the University of Minnesota (1946-1959) and the Harvard University (1959-1990).

He received the Nobel Prize in Chemistry for his work on boron chemistry and chemical bonding.

He died in 2011 at Cambridge, Massachusetts.

168. Donald James Cram (1919 – 2001)

Donald James Cram was an American chemist born in 1919 at Chester, Vermont. He shared the 1987 Nobel Prize in Chemistry with Charles J Pedersen and Marie Lehn for the development and use of molecules with structure-specific interactions of high selectivity. These people are responsible for the development of host-guest chemistry.

He studied his Master's degree at the University of Nebraska–Lincoln and doctoral degree at the Harvard University. Later, he worked at Merck and Co laboratories. He worked as a postdoctoral fellow at the Massachusetts Institute of Technology.

Cram is remembered for the introduction of Cram's rule which is used to deduce the outcome of nucleophilic attack to carbonyl compounds. He published around 350 articles and eight books.

He died in 2001 at the age of 82.

169. Rosalind E Franklin (1920 – 1958)

Rosalind Elsie Franklin was a British chemist born in 1920 at Notting Hill. Basically she was a X-ray crystallographer and worked for the understanding of the structures of DNA, RNA, coal, viruses, graphite. Her works on viruses and coal were recognized well in her life time but her work on discovery of DNA was unrecognized.

She was graduated from Newnham College in 1941. She worked at the British Coal Utilisation Research Association and obtained PhD degree from Cambridge in 1945. She worked as a postdoctoral researcher in France on X-ray cryatallography. Later, she joined to King's College, London in 1951 as research associate and moved to Birkbeck College in 1953.

She died in 1958 at Chelsea.

170. Peter Dennis Mitchell (1920 – 1992)

Peter Dennis Mitchell was a British chemist born in 1920 at Mitcham. He received the Nobel Prize in Chemistry in 1978 for his theory on ATP synthesis.

He received PhD degree from the Cambridge in 1951 for his work on the mode of action of penicillin. Later, he worked at the University of Edinburgh.

He died in 1992 at the age of 71.

171. George Porter (1920 – 2002)

George Porter was a British chemist born in 1920 at Stainforth. He received the Nobel Prize in Chemistry in 1967.

He did his research at the University of Cambridge under the guidance of Ronald George Wreyford Norrish. He worked as an assistant director of the British Rayon Research Association (1953-1954). He was a professor of chemistry at the University of Sheffield (1954-1965), where he worked on flash photolysis. Later, he became the director of the Royal Institution in 1966, where he worked on photophysics. Along with Manfred Eigen and Ronald George Wreyford Norrish, he was awarded the Nobel Prize in Chemistry in 1967.

He was a visiting professor at the University College London. He attempted to understand science to public. He was the president of the British Association in 1985. He gave the Romanes lecture, Dimbleby lecture and Gresham lectures.

He was a fellow of the Royal Society, member of the American Academy of Arts and Sciences and American Philosophical Society. He served as the president of the Royal Society. He received Davy, Rumford, Ellison-CLiffe and Copley medals.

He died in 2002 at the age of 81.

172. Geoffrey Wilkinson (1921 – 1996)

Geoffrey Wilkinson was an English chemist born in 1921 at Todmorden. He was a recipient of the Nobel Prize in Chemistry for his pioneering work on inorganic chemistry and homogeneous transition metal catalysis.

He worked with Prof. Friedrich Paneth on nuclear energy project in 1942. He worked in Canada as well at Montreal and Chalk River Laboratories in 1946. Later, he worked with Prof. Glenn Seaborg at the University of California, Berkeley on nuclear taxonomy. Then, he joined Massachusetts Institute of Technology as research associate. After working at the Harvard University, he returned to England in 1955. Finally, he became a faculty at the Imperial College London, where he worked on complexes of transition metals.

He was popular for the discovery of $RhCl(PPh_3)_3$, which is known as Wilkinson's catalyst. He also discovered the structure of ferrocene.

He died in 1996 at the age of 75.

173. Robert B Merrifield (1921 – 2006)

Robert Bruce Merrifield was an American chemist born in 1921 at Fort Worth, Texas to George E. Merrifield and Lorene née Lucas. He received 1984 Nobel Prize in Chemistry for the invention of solid phase peptide synthesis.

He was graduated from University of California at Los Angeles. Later, he worked at the Philip R. Park Research Foundation. Again he joined the same university and worked with Prof. M. S. Dunn. Then, he moved to the Rockefeller Institute for Medical Research at New York. Here, he invented solid phase peptide synthesis and published in Journal of the American Chemical Society. He synthesized bradykinin, angiotensin, desamino-oxytocin, insulin and ribonuclease A. He died in 2006 at the age of 84.

174. George S Hammond (1921 – 2005)

George Simms Hammond was an American chemist born in 1921 at Auburn. He was a theoretical chemist who developed 'Hammond's postulate'. He is considered as the father of organic photochemistry. He proposed the formation of transition state in an organic chemical reaction.

He received doctoral degree from the Harvard University in 1947. He worked as a postdoctoral fellow at the University of California, Los Angeles. He worked as a chemist at the California Institute of Technology. Besides, he extended his research work to the University of Oxford and University of Basel.

He received the Norris Award, Priestley Medal, National Medal of Science and Othmer Gold Medal.

He died in 2005 at the age of 84.

175. Isabella Karle (1921 – 2017)

Isabella Karle was an American chemist born in 1921 at Detroit, Michigan. She is well known for the extraction of plutonium chloride from a mixture containing plutonium oxide.

She studied at the University of Michigan for BSc, MSc and PhD degree. She worked for Manhattan Project at the time of World War II. Later, she joined the United States Naval Research Laboratory. She developed new interpretation methods for X-ray crystallographic data to get molecular structures.

She received Gregori Aminoff Prize, Garvan-Olin Medal, National Medal of Sciencce, Bower Award and the Navy Distinguished Civlian Service Award. She was a fellow of the National Academy of Sciences, the American Academy of Arts and Sciences and American Philosophical Society. Besides, she received many honorary doctorates.

She died in 2017 at the age of 95.

176. John B Goodenough (1922-2023)

John Bannister Goodenough was an American chemist born in 1922 at Jena, Germany. Basically, he was a materials chemist worked on solid state chemistry. He received the Nobel Prize in Chemistry. He became popular by devising Goodenough-Kanamori rules of the sign of the magnetic super exchange in materials.

He studied at the Yale University. Later, he served as meteorologist in the US military during the time of World War II. He received the PhD degree from the University of Chicago. He was a researcher at the MIT Lincoln lab and served as the head of the Inorganic chemistry lab at the University of Oxford. He was a professor of mechanical, electrical engineering and materials science at the University of Texas at Austin. He received many medals and prizes.

He died in 2023 at the age of 100.

177. Rudolph A Marcus (1923)

Rudolph Arthur Marcus is a Canadian born US chemist born in 1923 at Montreal to Esther and Myer Marcus. He received the Nobel Prize in Chemistry in 1992 for his work on theory of electron transfer reactions in chemical systems.

He studied at the McGill University to obtain his doctoral degree. Later, he worked at the National Research Council. Then, he joined the University of North Carolina and Polytechnic Institute of Brooklyn. Finally, he became a naturalized citizen of USA. He is a professor at Caltech and Nanyang Technological University, Singapore. He received honorary doctorate from many universities. Besides, he is a recipient of many awards. He is a member of the International Academy of Quantum Molecular Science, National Academy of Sciences, American Academy of Arts and Sciences, Royal Society of Chemistry, Canada.

178. Walter Kohn (1923 – 2016)

Walter Kohn was an Austrian-American chemist born in 1923 at Vienna. He received the 1998 Nobel Prize in Chemistry for his contributions to understand electronic properties of materials. He is instrumental in the development of density functional theory, which leads to understand quantum mechanical electronic structures.

He entered UK as a refugee during the time of World War II and then went to Canada in 1940 after the war. He studied MA in applied mathematics at the University of Toronto in 1945. He received doctoral degree from the Harvard University. He worked at the Carnegie Mellon University from 1950 to 1960 on multiple scattering band structure work and semiconductors. In 1960, he moved to the University of California, San Diego and worked on Fermi gas. He established Institute for Theoretical Physics in Santa Barbara. In 1984, he moved to the University of California at Santa Barbara as physics professor.

He died in 2016 at the age of 93.

179. Hugh Longuet-Higgins (1923 – 2004)

Hugh Christopher Longuet-Higgins was a British chemist born in 1923 at Lenham to Henry Hugh Longuet Longuet-Higgins and Albinia Cecil Bazeley. He was a theoretical chemist who worked at the University of Cambridge and the University of Edinburgh. He worked in the area of cognitive science. He made novel contributions to understand molecular science. He was instrumental in the establishment of the journal Molecular Physics.

While studying undergraduate course he proposed the correct bridged structure of diborane (B_2H_6). He received doctoral degree from the University of Oxford. He worked as a postdoctoral fellow at the University of Chicago and the University of Manchester. Later, he joined King's College London and then moved to the University of Cambridge.

He died in 2004 at the age of 80.

180. Ronald Gillespie (1924-2021)

Ronald James Gillespie was a British chemist born in 1924 at London. He worked on molecular geometry. In Canada, he was responsible for the establishment of inorganic chemistry education. He extensively worked on Valence Shell Electron Pair Repulsion theory. Besides, he also proposed Ligand Close Packing theory. He tried to interprete the covalent radius of fluorine.

He studied BSc, PhD and DSc at the University of London. He joined University College, London as lecturer. In 1958, he moved to McMaster University, Canada.

He was a fellow of the Royal Society of Canada, Royal Society of London and Order of Canada.

He died in 2021 at the age of 96.

181. John Anthony Pople (1925 – 2004)

John Anthony Pople was a British chemist born in 1925 at Burnham-on-Sea. He received the 1998 Nobel Prize in Chemistry for the development of computational methods in quantum chemistry.

He studied at Trinity College, Cambridge for Bachelor's degree. He worked at the Bristol Aeroplane Company between 1945 and 1947. He returned to the University of Cambridge to pursue PhD on lone pair electrons. He was a research fellow at the Trinity College. He worked as a mathematics faculty at Cambridge. He moved to the National Physical Laboratory in 1958. In 1964, he moved to USA, where he spent the rest of his life. He shifted to Carnegie Mellon University, Pittsburgh in 1964. In 1993, he moved to Northwestern University, Illinois, where he was a Trustees Professor of Chemistry until his death.

He died in 2004 at the age of 78.

182. Luis Cárdenas (1925 – 2004)

Luis Ernesto Miramontes Cárdenas was a Mexican chemist born in 1925 at Tepic. He was the firs to synthesize an oral contraceptive progestin norethisterone.

He received a degree in chemical engineering from the Universidad Nacional Autónoma de México. He was a founder researcher of this institute. He served as a professor of chemistry in the same institute. In addition, he served as the director and professor at the Universidad Iberoamericana, and deputy director of research at the Mexican Institute of Petroleum.

He was a member of the American Chemical Society, the National Institute of Chemical Engineers, the Mexican Institute of Chemical Engineers and the New York Academy of Sciences.

He died in 2004 at Mexico City at the age of 79.

183. Robert J P Williams (1926 – 2015)

Robert Joseph Paton Williams was a British chemist born in 1926 at Wallasey.

He studied at the Merton College, Oxford.

He was an emeritus fellow at Wadham College and Emeritus Professor at the University of Oxford. For his bachelor's degree we worked with Harry Irving on transition metal complexes. He completed DPhil in 1950. He worked on protein purification and developed a new method called gradient elution analysis. He joined Wadham College, Oxford in 1955 and worked there for the rest of his life.

His work on inorganic chemistry led to a two volume text book. In later stages, he developed interest on enzyme catalysis. He contributed to understand the distribution of the chemical elements in living organisms. He retired in 1991 and dedicated the rest of his life to write books.

He died in 2015 at the age of 89.

184. Paul Berg (1926-2023)

Paul Berg was an American chemist born in 1926 at New York City to Sarah Brodsky and Harry Berg. He was a professor at Stanford University. He received the 1980 Nobel Prize in chemistry for his work on nucleic acids, in particular recombinant DNA.

He did his undergraduation at Penn State University. He received PhD degree from the Western Reserve University. He worked as a professor at Washington University School of Medicine and Stanford University School of Medicine. Besides, he was the director of the Beckman Center for Molecular and Genetic Medicine.

In addition to the Nobel prize, he was a recipient of National Medal of Science and National Library of Medicine Medal.

He died in 2023 at Stanford at the age of 96.

185. Aaron Klug (1926 – 2018)

Aaron Klug was a British chemist born in 1926 at Zelva to Lazar and Bella Klug. He was a recipient of 1982 Nobel Prize in Chemistry for his contribution on crystallographic electron microscopy and structural elucidation of nucleic acid-protein complexes.

He got elementary education at the Durban High School. At this age, he developed interest in microbiology. He received bachelor's degree from the University of the Witwaters and master's degree from the University of Cape Town and doctoral degree from Trinity College, Cambridge. Later, he joined Birkbeck College, where he worked with Rosalind Franklin and John Bernal on crystallography. He discovered the structure of tobacco mosaic virus. He studied the structure of transfer RNA. In 1962, he became a fellow of Peterhouse, Cambridge and an honorary fellow.

He died in 2018 at the age of 92.

186. Irwin Allan Rose (1926 – 2015)

Irwin Allan Rose was an American scientist born in 1926 at Brooklyn to Ella (Greenwald) and Harry Royze. He received the Nobel Prize in chemistry in 2004 for the discovery of ubiquitin-mediated protein degradation.

He was in Washington State University before World War II. After the war, he did his BSc and PhD from the University of Chicago. He was a postdoctoral fellow at the New York University.

He worked at Yale School of Medicine, Fox Chase Cancer Center, University of Pennsylvania and University of California, Irvine School of Medicine.

He died in 2015 at the age of 88.

187. Manfred Eigen (1927-2019)

Manfred Eigen was a German chemist born in 1927 at Bochum to Hedwig (Feld) and Ernst Eigen. He received the Nobel Prize in Chemistry in 1967 for his work on fast chemical reactions. He contributed to solve problems in physical chemistry and to understand biological chemical reactions. Besides, he also worked to explore

biochemical roots of life and evolution. He is responsible for the establishment of new branch in science 'biotechnology'. He served German army during World War II. He was captured by Soviet army and he escaped to Göttingen in 1945. He was not allowed to enter the universities because of lack of required documents. After demonstrating his knowledge and talent in examinations, he was admitted. He worked under Werner Heisenberg. He completed PhD degree in 1951 from University of Göttingen. He demonstated his findings on fast reactions at the Faraday Society, London. He worked at the Max Planck Institute and Max Planck Institute for Biophysical Chemistry. He was a honorary professor at the Braunschweig University of Technology. He died in 2019.

188. George Andrew Olah (1927 – 2017)

George Andrew Olah was a Hungarian born American chemist born in 1927 at Budapest. He received 1994 Nobel Prize in Chemistry for his work on generation and reactivity of carbocations.

In 1956, after the Hungarian Revolution, he migrated to the UK. Then he moved to Canada in 1964. Finally, he settled in USA in 1965. He studied at the Technical University of Budapest for his master's and doctoral degree. He worked as a professor and director at the Hungarian Academy of Sciences. Later, he joined Dow Chemical in Canada. He joined Case Western Reserve University, USA. Finally, he served at the University of Southern California.

He also received Priestley Medal and F. A. Cotton Medal. He died in 2017 at the age of 89.

189. Frank S Rowland (1927 – 2012)

Frank Sherwood Rowland was an American chemist born in 1927 at Delaware. He was a Nobel laureate for his discovery of ozone depletion by chlorofluorocarbons. He was a professor at the University of California, Irvine.

He studied at the Ohio Wesleyan University, University of Chicago. He received PhD in 1952. He worked at Princeton University (1952-56), University of Kansas (1956-64) and University of California, Irvine (from 1964).

He was elected to National Acamedy of Sciences in 1978; he was a president of American Association for the Advancement of Science.

He died in 2012 at the age of 84.

190. Alan G MacDiarmid (1927 – 2007)

Alan Graham MacDiarmid was a New Zealand born American chemist born in 1927 at Masterton. He recived the Nobel Prize in Chemistry in 2000 for his work on conductive polymers.

He developed interest in chemistry at the age of ten by reading books. He was educated at the Victoria University of Wellington for BSc degree. Later, he worked as demonstrator in the undergraduate laboratories. He received MSc degree also from the same university and worked as an assistant in chemistry department. He published his first article in 1949 in the journal Nature. In 1951, he got Fulbright Fellowship to study at the University of Wisconsin–Madison for PhD degree. He got his second doctoral degree at the Sidney Sussex College, Cambridge in 1955. He worked at the University of St Andrews in Scotland and then he joined the University of Pennsylvania, where he worked for 45 years. In 2002, he joined the University of Texas at Dallas.

He died in 2007 at the age of 79.

191. Osamu Shimomura (1928 – 2018)

Osamu Shimomura was a Japanese chemist born in 1928 at Fukuchiyama. He won 2008 Nobel Prize in chemistry for his work on green fluorescent protein.

He was an emeritus professor at Marine Biological Laboratory in Woods Hole, Massachusetts and Boston University School of Medicine.

He studied BS degree at the College of Pharmaceutical Sciences of Nagasaki Medical College and stayed as lab assistant till 1955. Later, he joined Nagoya University in 1956 as an assistant to Prof. Yoshimasa Hirata, where he obtained MS and PhD degrees. He went to the Princeton University in 1960 to work with Prof. Frank Johnson. He died in 2018 at the age of 90 at Nagasaki.

192. Elias James Corey (1928-)

Elias James Corey was an American chemist born in 1928 at Methuen, Massachusetts.

He received the Nobel Prize in Chemistry in 1990 for his work on theory and methodology of organic synthesis.

He introduced retrosynthetic analysis. He has developed many reagents, methodologies and total syntheses.

He entered MIT to get BSc and PhD degrees. Initially, he was interested in mathematics. But, later attending his first chemistry class, he developed interest in chemistry and graduated in it.

He was offered by University of Illinois at Urbana–Champaign for a faculty position in 1956. In 1959, he shifted to Harvard University.

He has received many medals and prizes in addition to the Nobel Prize.

193. John Charles Polanyi (1929-)

John Charles Polanyi was a German-born Canadian chemist born in 1929 at Berlin.

In 1986, he won the Nobel Prize in Chemistry for his work on chemical kinetics.

He came from a poor family which migrated to UK where he was educated at the University of Manchester.

He did his postdocotoral research at National Research Council, Canada and Princeton University, New Jersey.

He was appointed to the University of Toronto, where he is currently working.

He has received many medals, prizes and honorary degrees in addition to the Nobel Prize.

194. Paul C Lauterbur (1929 – 2007)

Paul Christian Lauterbur was an American chemist born in 1929 at Sidney, Ohio. He received the 2003 Nobel Prize in Physiology or Medicine for the development of magnetic resonance imaging (MRI).

He built his own laboratory in his home during teenage because of his interest in the subject. He was educated at the Case Institute of Technology. He served US army as well during 1950s, where he woked with early NMR machine and published four articles on that.

He was a professor at the Stony Brook University between 1963 and 1985, where he started developing MRI. He moved to University of Illinois at Urbana-Champaign and stayed here for the rest of his life.

He died in 2007 at the age of 77.

195. John Kenneth Stille (1930 – 1989)

John Kenneth Stille was an American chemist born in 1930 at Tucson, Arizona. He is well known for the invention of Stille coupling reaction, which involves the reaction between stannanes and aryl halides to get biaryls catalyzed by palladium.

He studied at the University of Arizona to receive BA and MA degrees. He served US army as well during Korean War. He did his PhD at the University of Illinois under the guidance of Carl Shipp Marvel.

He worked at the University of Iowa, the Colorado State University and the University of Arizona.

He died in the United Airlines Flight 232 crash at Soiux City, Iowa at the age of 59.

196. Stanley Lloyd Miller (1930 – 2007)

Stanley Lloyd Miller was an American chemist born in 1930 at Oakland. He is well known for the Miller-Urey experiment, which demonstrates the formation of organic molecules from inorganic precursors. This experiment is helpful in understanding the origin of life.

He studied at the University of California at Berkeley and completed BSc in 1951. After his father's death in 1946, he experienced money shortage. This led him to work as teaching assistant at the University of Chicago. He enrolled to PhD degree in 1951 at the University of Chicago under the guidance of Edward Teller. After obtaining doctoral degree, he moved to California Institute of Technology and worked on synthesis of amino and hydroxycarboxylic acids. Next he shifted to Columbia University, New York followed by accepting the assistant professor position at the University of California at San Diego, where he served as associate professor and professor as well. He guided many doctoral students and authored a book 'The Origin of Life on Earth'.

He died in 2007 at the age of 77.

197. Frank Albert Cotton (1930 – 2007)

Frank Albert Cotton was an American chemist born in 1930 at Philadelphia. His work on chemistry of transition metals gave him a great recognition.

He studied at the Drexel University and Temple University. After obtaining BA degree he joined Prof. Geoffrey Wilkinson's lab at the Harvard University, where he conducted research on metallocenes. Later, he started his career at Massachusetts Institute of Technology. He was a distinguished professor at the Texas A&M University.

He died in 2007 at the age of 77.

198. Dewan Singh Bhakuni (1930-2021)

Dewan Singh Bhakuni was an Indian chemist born in 1930 in Uttar Pradesh. He worked in the area of natural products and stereochemistry.

He studied at the Allahabad University for BSc and MSc. He joined Central Drug Research Institute in 1959. He next moved to the National Botanical Research Institute in 1962. Later, he went to UK to pursue PhD degree in 1965. He received doctoral degree from the University of London under the supervision of Derek Barton on the topic *'Studies in alkaloid biosynthesis'*. He also received DSc from the same university in 1978.

He was a scientist at Central Drug Research Institute. He was a Fellow of Indian Academy of Sciences, National Academy of Sciences and Indian National Science Academy. He received the Shanti Swarup Bhatnagar Prize for Science and Technology in 1975.

He died in 2021 at the age of 90.

199. Akira Suzuki (1930-)

Akira Suzuki is a Japanese chemist born in 1930 at Mukawa. He is a recipient of 2010 Nobel Prize in Chemistry for the invention of Suzuki reaction, which involves reaction between boronic acids with aryl halides catalyzed by palladium complexes. He invented this reaction in 1979.

He studied at the Hokkaido University and worked at the same university as assistant professor. Although he was interested to major in mathematics, he majored chemistry because he was influenced by the books written by Louis Fieser and Herbert C. Brown. He did his postdoctoral research at the Purdue University under Herbert C. Brown. On returning to Japan, he occupied a professor position in Hokudai, where he invented the Suzuki reaction.

200. Yves Chauvin (1930 – 2015)

Yves Chauvin was a French chemist born in 1930 at Menen, Belgium. He was a recipient of 2005 Nobel Prize in Chemistry for his work on olefin metathesis.

He was graduated from the Ecole supérieure de chimie physique électronique de Lyon in 1954. Later, he worked in a chemical factory and he got frustrated there. In 1960, he joined French Petroleum Institute and worked there even after the retirement. Besides, he was also an emeritus director of Lyon School of Chemistry, Physics, and Electronics.

He was a member of the French Academy of Sciences.

He died in 2015 at the age of 84.

201. Martin Karplus (1930-)

Martin Karplus is an Austrian-born American chemist born in 1930 at Vienna. He won 2013 Nobel Prize in Chemistry for his work on multiscale models for complex chemical systems.

He was educated at the Harvard College and California Institute of Technology. He received doctoral degree in 1953 under the guidance of Nobel laureate Linus Pauling. He did postdoctoral research at the University of Oxford under Prof. Charles Coulson.

He began his teaching career at the University of Illinois at Urbana–Champaign (1955-1960) and then continued at the Columbia University (1960-1965). Finally he settled at the Harvard in 1966. He was also a professor at the Louis Pasteur University at France.

He is the Director of the Biophysical Chemistry Laboratory. He is a Theodore William Richards Professor and emeritus professor at the Harvard University. He has guided more than 200 graduate students including postdoctoral researchers since 1955.

202. Richard F Heck (1931 – 2015)

Richard Frederick Heck was an American chemist born in 1931 at Springfield, Massachusetts. He is well known for the invention of Heck reaction, which involves the reaction between aryl halides and alkenes catalyzed by palladium. He received the Nobel Prize in Chemistry in 2010 for this work.

He studied at the University of California, Los Angeles for BSc degree and PhD degree under the guidance of Saul Winstein. He was a postdoctoral fellow at the ETH, Zurich, Switzerland in Vladimir Prelog's lab. He returned to the University of California, Los Angeles. He worked on polymer chemistry at the Hercules Corporation in Wilmington.

He died in 2015 at the age of 84.

203. Walter Gilbert (1932-)

Walter Gilbert is an American scientist born in 1931 at Boston.

He studied at the Harvard University for undergraduate and graduate studies. He entered the University of Cambridge to pursue PhD degree under the guidance of Nobel laureate Abdus Salam. He returned to Harvard in 1956 and worked as an assistant professor, associate professor and professor.

He is a co-founder of a biotech company Biogen. He left Harvard to lead Biogen as CEO. He is a member of The Scripps Research Institute and chairman of Harvard Society of Fellows. He started another company named Paratek Pharmaceuticals in 1996, served as its chairman until 2014.

He received many awards namely Harvard's Ledlie Prize, Louisa Gross Horwitz Prize, Gairdner Prize and 1980 Nobel Prize in Chemistry for determining the sequence of nucleotides in nucleic acids.

204. Dudley R Herschbach (1932-)

Dudley Robert Herschbach is an American chemist born in 1932 at San Jose, California. He received the Nobel Prize in Chemistry in 1986 for his work on dynamics of chemical processes. He worked on crossed molecular beam that helped in understanding elementary reactions.

He got BS and MS degrees at the Stanford University. He received PhD degree from the Harvard University in 1958 under the guidance of Edgar Bright Wilson on exmination of tunnel splitting in molecules by employing microwave spectroscopy. Later, he joined the University of California at Berkeley as an assistant professor. He was promoted to associate professor in 1961. In 1963, he returned to Harvard as professor. He has published around 400 research articles. He has broad expertise both in chemistry and physics.

He is a fellow of the National Academy of Sciences, the American Academy of Arts and Sciences, the American Philosophical Society and the Royal Chemical Society. He has received many more awards like the National Medal of Science, the Linus Pauling Medal, the ACS Award in Pure Chemistry, the Irving Langmuir Award and the American Institute of Chemists Gold Medal.

205. Michael Smith (1932-2000)

Michael Smith was a British-born Canadian chemist born in 1932 at Blackpool. He won 1993 Nobel Prize in Chemistry for developing site-directed mutagenesis.

He received doctoral degree from the University of Manchester in 1956 followed by postdoctoral research at Nobel laurete Har Gobind Khorana's lab at Vancouver, Canada.

Later, he worked at the Fisheries Research Board of Canada Laboratory and UBC Faculty of Medicine.

He died in 2000 at the age of 68.

206. Richard Robert Ernst (1933-2021)

Richard Robert Ernst was a Swiss chemist born in 1933 at Winterthur to Robert Ernst and Irma Ernst-Brunner. He was a recipient of 1991 Nobel Prize in Chemistry for his work on developemnt of Fourier transform nuclear magnetic resonance spectroscopy (FT-NMR).

He received diploma in chemistry in 1957 at Eidgenössische Technische Hochschule (ETH). He self studied quantum mechanics and thermodynamics in spare time. After serving militaty, he received PhD in chemistry in 1962 from ETH.

He worked at Varian Associates in 1963 as a scientist and developed FT-NMR. He returned to ETH and served there as assiatant professor, associate professor and professor. He retired in 1998. He was a fellow to many academic bodies, received many awards and medals.

He died in 2021 at the age of 87.

207. Paul Jozef Crutzen (1933-2021)

Paul Jozef Crutzen was a Dutch chemist born in 1933 at Amsterdam to Anna (Gurk) and Josef Crutzen. He received 1995 Nobel Prize in Chemistry for his work on formation and decomposition of ozone in atmosphere. He introduced the term nuclear winter which describe the effects of forest fires, industrial exhausts and other oil fires.

He was graduated in 1951. Atmospheric chemistry was his primary research area. He is well known for his research on ozone depletion.

He was a member of the Royal Swedish Academy of Sciences and Royal Soceity of UK.

He died in 2021 at the age of 87.

208. Robert Floyd Curl Jr. (1933-2022)

Robert Floyd Curl Jr. was an American chemist born in 1933 at Alice, Texas. He worked at the Rice University as Pitzer–Schlumberger Professor of Natural Sciences and Chemistry. He was the recipient of 1996 Nobel Prize in Chemistry for the discovery of buckminsterfullerene: a nano material.

He was educated with a BSc degree from the Rice Institute in 1954. He received PhD from the University of California, Berkeley in 1957, where he worked with Kenneth Pitzer who was his lifelong collaborator. He worked on determination of bond angle of disiloxane using infrared spectroscopy. He was a postdoctoral fellow at the Harvard University in E B Wilson's lab, where he worked on bond rotation barriers of molecules using microwave spectroscopy. Later, he joined Rice University in 1958.Initially he worked on microwave spectra of chlorine dioxide. Besides, he focused on detection and analysis of free radicals using microwave spectroscopy and lasers.

He died in 2022 at the age of 88 at Houston, Texas.

209. C. N. R. Rao (1934-)

Chintamani Nagesa Ramachandra Rao is an Indian chemist born in 1934 at Bangalore. He is working on solid state and structural chemistry. He studied BSc at the University of Mysore, MSc at the Banaras Hindu University, PhD at the Purdue University. Later, he joined Indian Institute of Science (IISc) as lecturer in 1959. He moved to Indian Institute of Technology Kanpur. He returned to IISc and served as its director (1984-1994). He was chief of the Scientific Advisory Council to the Prime Minister of India (1985-1989 and 2005-2014). He has received honorary doctorates from 86 universities, published 1800 research articles and authored in 56 books.

He founded and works in Jawaharlal Nehru Centre for Advanced Scientific Research.

210. Ei-ichi Negishi (1935-2021)

Ei-ichi Negishi was a Japanese chemist born in 1935 at Xinjing. He is well known for the invention of Negeshi coupling, which involves palladium catalyzed cross coupling of aryl halides with organozinc compounds. He received the Nobel Prize in Chemistry in 2010 for this work.

He was educated at the University of Tokyo. He received PhD from the University of Pennsylvania in 1963 under the guidance of Prof. Allan R Day. He was a postdoctoral fellow at the Purdue University. He entered to indepenent academic career at Syracuse University as an assistant professor. He returned to Purdue University as professor in 1979. He retired in 2019. He published around 400 research articles.

He died in 2021 at the age of 85 at Indianapolis.

211. Yuan Tseh Lee (1936-)

Yuan Tseh Lee is a Taiwanese chemist born in 1936 at Shinchiku City. He is a recipient of 1986 Nobel Prize in Chemistry for his work on dynamics of chemical elelmentary processes. He used advanced chemical kinetics methods to understand the behavior of chemical reactions using crossed molecular beams.

He studied BSc at National Taiwan University, MSc at National Tsing Hua University and PhD at University of California, Berkeley. He was a postdoctoral fellow at the Harvard University. Later, he joined the University of Chicago in 1968. In 1974, he moved to Berkeley as professor of chemistry.

He is an emeritus professor at the University of California, Berkeley.

He served as the President of the Academia Sinica of Taiwan. He was the head of the International Council for Science.

He was a member of the Chemistry International Board.

212. Alan Jay Heeger (1936-)

Alan Jay Heeger is an American chemist born in 1936 at Sioux City, Iowa. He received the Nobel Prize in Chemistry in 2000 for the discovery of conductive polymers. He prepared polyacetylene in 1977.

He studied BSc at the University of Nebraska-Lincoln and PhD in the University of California, Berkeley. He was a faculty of the University of Pennsylvania and the University of California, Santa Barbara. His research led to the establishment of many companies.

He is a member of National Academy of Engineering. He has won Oliver E. Buckley Prize and Balzan Prize.

213. Hideki Shirakawa (1936-)

Hideki Shirakawa is a Japanese chemist born in 1936 at Tokyo. He received the Nobel Prize in Chemistry in 2000 for the discovery of conductive polymers.

He was educated at the Tokyo Institute of Technology. He was an assistant in chemical resources laboratory in Tokyo Tech, where he developed polyacetylene. This attracted Alan MacDiarmid to visit Tokyo Tech in 1975. In 1976, he got an opportunity to work in MacDiarmid lab as postdoctoral fellow at the University of Pennsylvania. In 1979, he joined the University of Tsukuba as assistant professor and later promoted as professor.

They developed electrical conductivity in polyacetylene along with American scientist Alan Jay Heeger. They found that electrical conductivity of polyacetylene can be increased when it is doped with iodine. These three scientists received the Nobel Prize in Chemistry in 2000.

He is a Emeritus Professor at the University of Tsukuba and Zhejiang University.

214. Gerhard Ertl (1936-)

Gerhard Ertl is a German chemist born in 1936 at Stuttgart. He laid foundation for the modern surface chemistry, which helped to understand how fuel cells produce energy without pollution. His research helped for the development of cleaner energy sources. For this work, he received the Nobel Prize in Chemistry in 2007.

He was educated at the Technical University of Stuttgart, University of Paris, Ludwig Maximilian University, Max Planck Institute for Metals Research and Technical University of Munich. After receiving doctoral degree, he joined Technical University of Munich as lecturer (1965-68). He was the director and professor at the Technical University of Hannover (1968-73). He worked at Ludwig Maximilian University of Munich as professor (1973-86). He was a visiting professor at the California Institute of Technology, the University of Wisconsin–Milwaukee and the University of California, Berkeley. He was the director of Fritz Haber Institute of the MPG from 1986 till his retirement.

He is an emeritus professor at the Fritz-Haber-Institut der Max-Planck-Gesellschaft, Berlin.

215. Avram Hershko (1937-)

Avram Hershko is a Hungarian-Israeli scientist born in 1937 at Karcag, Hungary to Shoshana and Moshe Hershko. He is a recipient of 2004 Nobel Prize in Chemistry for his work on ubiquitin-mediated protein degradation.

He received his doctoral degree from the Hebrew University of Jerusalem. He was a postdoctoral fellow at the University of California, San Francisco.

Currently, he is a distinguished professor at the Technion, Haifa and adjunct professor at the New York University Grossman School of Medicine.

216. Roald Hoffmann (1937-)

Roald Hoffmann is a Polish born American chemist born in 1937 at Zloczow to Clara (Rosen) and Hillel Safran. He received the Nobel Prize in Chemistry in 1981 for the development of theories concerning the course of chemical reactions.

When he was a child, Germans invaded Poland and his family was imprisoned. They managed to escape from the extermination camps and hidden in a storeroom of the local school house for 18 months. But his father remained in the camp and he was killed by Germans later. His mother remarried a new man later and adopted his surname Hoffman. They migrated to USA in 1949. He received bachelor's degree from the Columbia University, masters and doctoral degree from the Harvard University. He worked on molecular orbital theory of polyhedral molecules. He extended Hückel method with Lawrence Lohr. In 1965, he moved to Cornell and spent the rest of his life there.

Currently, he is a emeritus professor at the Cornell University.

217. Robert Huber (1937-)

Robert Huber is a German chemist born in 1937 at Munich. He is a recipient of the Nobel Prize for his work on crystallizing a membrane protein which is involved in photosynthesis in purple bacteria and its structure determination using X-ray crystallography.

He studied chemistry at the Technische Hochschule and used crystallography to determine the structure of organic compounds. In 1971, he was the director of Max Planck Institute for Biochemistry, where he developed methods for the crystallization of proteins. He worked in Cardiff University as well. Since 2005, he is working at the *Center for medical biotechnology* of the University of Duisburg-Essen. He has received the Otto Warburg Zmedal in 1977. He was a member of Pour le Mérite for Sciences and Arts.

218. Ryoji Noyori (1938-)

Ryōji Noyori is a Japanese chemist born in 1938 at Kobe. He received 2001 Nobel Prize in Chemistry for his work on asymmetric hydrogenations.

He was graduated and postgraduated from Kyoto University. He also received Doctor of Engineering degree from the same university and got appointed there as an associate professor. He was a postdoctoral fellow at Harvard under E. J. Corey. Later, he returned to Nagoya as full professor in 1972. He is still working there and worked as the president of RIKEN.

He was an Honorary Doctor at the University of Rennes 1, the Technical University of Munich and RWTH Aachen University. He was elected as a foreign member of the Royal Society in 2005. He received an honorary doctorate from the Institute of Chemical Technology, Mumbai. He has received many awards and medals.

The Ryōji Noyori Prize is named in his honour.

219. Kurt Wüthrich (1938-)

Kurt Wüthrich is a Swiss chemist born in 1938 at Aarberg. He is a recipient of Nobel Prize in Chemistry for his work on developing nuclear magnetic resonance methods for studying biological macromolecules.

He studied physics, chemistry and mathematics at the University of Bern. He did his doctoral work at the University of Basel under the guidance of Silvio Fallab. He was a postdoctoral fellow at the University of California, Berkeley (1965-1967). He worked for Bell Telephone Laboratories (1967-1969). He returned to Switzerland and started work at the ETH Zürich. He also worked with The Scripps Research Institute and Shanghai Tech University. He is a visiting professor at the University of Edinburgh, Chinese University of Hong Kong and Yonsei University.

He has received many honours and awards.

220. Tomas R Lindahl (1938-)

Tomas Robert Lindahl is a Swedish-British scientist born in 1938 at Stockholm. He is specialized in cancer research. He is a recipient of 2015 Nobel Prize in Chemistry for his work on mechanistic studies of DNA repair.

He studied at Karolinska Institutet at Stockholm for PhD and MD degree. He was a postdoctoral fellow at the Princeton University and Rockefeller University. He was a professor at the University of Gothenburg (1978-1982). He moved to UK as a researcher at the Imperial Cancer Research Fund in 1981. He was the director of Clare Hall Laboratories (1986-2005). Since 2015, he is working at the Francis Crick Institute. He has published many articles on DNA repair and the genetics of cancer. He was a member of EMBO, Fellow of the Royal Society, member of the Norwegian Academy of Science and Letters, Fellow of the Academy of Medical Sciences and National Academy of Sciences. He received the Royal Medal in 2007 from the Royal Society.

221. Barbara S Askins (1939-)

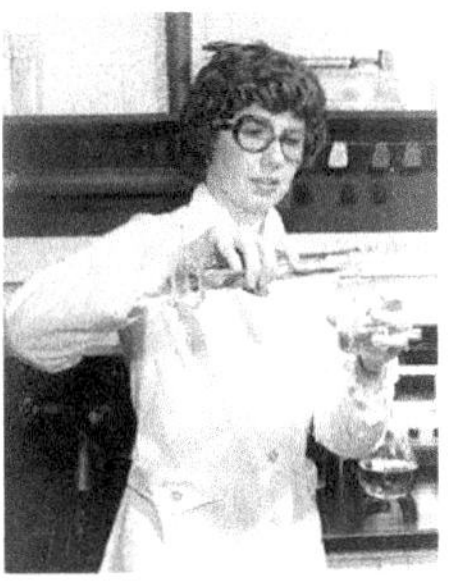

Barbara S. Askins is an American chemist born in 1939 at Belfast. She is well known for the invention of developing a method to enhance underexposed photographic negatives. This invention was used by NASA and the medical industry. She received the title of National Inventor of the year 1978 by the Association for Advancement of Inventions and Innovations. She was the first woman to receive this honor.

She started her career as a teacher and entered NASA's Marshall Space Flight Center in 1975. She developed autoradiograph to reproduce the image. This invention was also used to develop X-ray images in medical field. She patented this invention in 1978. She is a member of the American Chemical Society, the American Association for the Advancement of Science and the World Future Society.

222. Jean-Marie Lehn (1939-)

Jean-Marie Lehn is a French chemist born in 1939 at Rosheim. He is the recipient of 1987 Nobel Prize in Chemistry for his synthesis of cryptands. He is one of the early inventors in the area of supramolecular chemistry.

He studied at the University of Strasbourg for PhD degree under the guidance of Guy Ourisson. He did his postdoctoral work at the Harvard University in Robert Burns Woodward's lab, where he worked on the synthesis of vitamin B12. Later, he returned to Strasbourg as assistant professor in 1966. He was able to synthesize cage-like molecules called cryptands in 1968.

He has published 790 research articles as of 2006. Currently, he is a member of the Reliance Innovation Council, India.

223. Sidney Altman (1939-2022)

Sidney Altman was a Canadian-American scientist born in 1939 at Montreal to Arlin Ray and Victor Altman. He was married to Ann M Körner. He received 1989 Nobel Prize in Chemistry for his work on the catalytic properties of RNA.

He studied at the Massachusetts Institute of Technology and Columbia University, University of Colorado Medical Center (where he got PhD degree). He further studied at the Vanderbilt University and the Harvard University. At Harvard he worked with Matthew Meselson's lab on DNA endonuclease involved in the replication and recombination of T4 DNA.

He was the Sterling Professor of Molecular, Cellular, and Developmental Biology and Chemistry at Yale University. He was a fellow of the American Academy of Arts and Sciences and member of the National Academy of Sciences and American Philosophical Society. He died in 2022 at the age of 82.

224. Harold W Kroto (1939 – 2016)

Sir Harold Walter Kroto was a British chemist born in 1939 at Wisbech to Edith and Heinz Krotoschiner. He received the Nobel Prize in Chemistry in 1996 for the discovery of fullerenes. Besides, he received many awards and honors.

He studied at the University of Sheffield. He was interested in physics, chemistry and mathematics by the influence of Harry Heaney. He supported British Humanist Association.

He worked at the University of Sussex for 40 years. He was the Francis Eppes Professor of Chemistry at the Florida State University.

He died in 2016 at the age of 76.

225. Ada E Yonath (1939)

Ada E. Yonath is an Israeli chemist born in 1939 at Jerusalem to Hillel and Esther Lifshitz. Basically, she is a crystallographer and received the Nobel Prize in Chemistry in 2009 for her work on the structure of ribosomes. She is the first Israeli woman to win the Nobel Prize. She was inspired by Marie Curie.

She studied BSc at the Hebrew University of Jerusalem and PhD at the Weizmann Institute of Science under the supervision of Wolfie Traub. She was a postdoctoral fellow at the Carnegie Mellon University and MIT.

She established a protein crystallography lab in Israel in 1970. She was a group leader of Max Planck Institute for Molecular Genetics. She was a visiting professor at the University of Chicago. Besides, she worked with Max-Planck Institute also. She received many awards and prizes. Currently, she is the director of the Helen and Milton A. Kimmelman Center for Biomolecular Structure and Assembly of the Weizmann Institute of Science.

226. Thomas A Steitz (1940 – 2018)

Thomas Arthur Steitz was an American scientist born in 1940 at Milwaukee. He was a professor at Yale University and worked with Howard Hughes Medical Institute. He is well known for his research on ribosomes. He received the Nobel Prize in Chemistry in 2009 for studies on the function and structure of the ribosomes. He is also a recipient of the Gairdner International Award in 2007.

He studied bachelor's and doctoral degrees at the Lawrence University. He determined the structures of carboxypeptidase A and aspartate carbamoyltransferase. He was a postdoctoral fellow at the MRC Laboratory of Molecular Biology. He joined the University of California, Berkeley as assistant professor.

He was a Macy fellow at the University of Göttingen and Fairchild Scholar at the California Institute of Technology. He started a pharmaceutical company Rib-X for the development of novel antibiotics.

He died in 2018 at the age of 78.

227. Arieh Warshel (1940-)

Arieh Warshel is an Israeli born American scientist born in 1940 at Kibbutz Sde Nahum. He worked on computational studies related to functional properties of biomolecules. He is a recipient of 2013 Nobel Prize in Chemistry for developing multiscale models for complex chemical systems.

After serving Israeli army, he studied BSc at Technion, Haifa. Later, he studied MSc and PhD at Weizmann Institute of Science. He was a postdoctoral fellow at the Harvard University. He worked in Laboratory of Molecular Biology, UK.

He is a distinguished professor at the University of Southern California.

228. Joachim Frank (1940-)

Joachim Frank is a German-American chemist born in 1940 at Siegen, Germany. He received 2017 Nobel Prize in Chemistry for the invention of cryo-electron microscopy. He also determined the structure and function of ribosomes of eukaryotes and bacteria.

He studied at the Freiburg and Munich universities. He received doctoral degree from the Technical University of Munich in 1970. He worked across the globe including USA and Europe.

229. Karl Barry Sharpless (1941-)

Karl Barry Sharpless is an American chemist born in 1941 at Philadelphia. He received the Nobel Prize twice for the invention of stereoselective reactions (2001) and click chemistry (2022). He is one among five to receive the Nobel Prize twice.

He did his PhD at the Stanford University. He was a postdoctoral fellow at the Harvard University.

He worked at the Massachusetts Institute of Technology and Stanford University. At Stanford, he invented Sharpless asymmetric epoxidation. He worked at Scripps Research lab as well.

In 2001, he received his first Nobel Prize for the developemnt of Sharpless epoxidation, Sharpless asymmetric dihydroxylation and Sharpless oxyamination. In 2022, he again received the Nobel Prize for the invention of click chemistry.

He is a recipient of many awards including Priestley medal.

He is a distinguished professor at the Kyushu University. He received honorary degree from the KTH Royal Institute of Technology, Catholic University of Louvain, Technical University of Munich and Wesleyan University

230. George Pearson Smith (1941-)

George Pearson Smith is an American scientist born in 1941 at Norwalk. He received the Nobel Prize in Chemistry in 2018 for his work on phage display of peptides and antibodies.

He studied at Harvard University for doctoral degree. He was a postdoctoral fellow at the University of Wisconsin. In 1975, he joined the University of Missouri as a faculty. He also worked at Duke University with Robert Webster, where he started working on ideas which brought him the Nobel Prize.

Currently, he is an emeritus professor at the University of Missouri.

231. John Ernest Walker (1941-)

Sir John Ernest Walker is a British chemist born in 1941 at Halifax to Thomas Ernest Walker Elsie Lawton. He received the Nobel Prize in Chemistry in 1997.

He studied BA degree at the St Catherine's College. He worked with Edward Abraham at Oxford on peptide antibiotics to get doctoral degree in 1969. He became interested in molecular biology during this time.

Between 1969 and 1971, he worked for the University of Wisconsin–Madison and between 1971 and 1974, he worked at France. He later, worked at the Laboratory of Molecular Biology of Medical Research Council. He worked on crystallographic studies of the F1-ATPase.

He has guided number of students and received many awards and honours. Currently, he is an emeritus director and professor at the MRC Mitochondrial Biology Unit and a fellow of Sidney Sussex College.

232. Dan Shechtman (1941-)

Dan Shechtman is an Israeli chemist born in 1941 at Tel Aviv. He won the Nobel Prize in Chemistry in 2011 for the discovery of quasicrystals. He is the sixth Israeli citizen to win the Nobel Prize.

He received BSc, MSc and PhD degrees from the Technion in 1966, 1968 and 1972 respectively.

He is the Philip Tobias Professor at the Technion – Israel Institute of Technology. His works are in association with US Department of Energy. He holds a professorship at Iowa State University. When he was working for U.S. National Bureau of Standards, he discovered quasicrystals.

Since 2014, he is the head of the ISC (International Scientific Council) of Tomsk Polytechnic University.

233. Michael S Whittingham (1941-)

Michael Stanley Whittingham is a Britain born American chemist born in 1941 at Nottingham. He received the Nobel Prize in Chemistry in 2019 for his work on lithium-ion batteries.

He studied BA, MA and DPhil at the University of Oxford in 1964, 1967 and 1968 respectively. Later, he worked as a postdoctoral fellow at the Stanford University. He worked at Exxon Research & Engineering Company and Schlumberger before moving to Binghamton University as professor. He served as the vice-chair of State University of New York's the Research Foundation.

He is working as a professor at the Binghamton University and State University of New York. He is also serving as the director of the NECCES (Northeastern Center for Chemical Energy Storage) of the US. Department of Energy. At Binghamton University, he is a distinguished professor of materials science and engineering.

234. James F Stoddart (1942-)

Sir James Fraser Stoddart is a Britain born American chemist born in 1942 at Edinburgh to Tom and Jean Stoddart. He is working on nanotechnology and supramolecular chemistry. He has developed synthetic methods for mechanically-interlocked molecular  architectures like catenanes, molecular Borromean rings and rotaxanes. These topologies can be used as molecular switches. He also works on nanoelectromechanical systems and nanoelectronic devices. He is a recipient of the 2016 Nobel Prize in Chemistry for the design and synthesis of molecular machines.

He studied BSc and PhD degrees at the University of Edinburgh. He was a postdoctoral fellow at the Queen's University, Canada. He was a research fellow at the University of Sheffield. He was a visiting fellow at the University of California, Los Angeles. He moved to ICI Corporate Laboratory in 1978 and to Sheffield in 1982. He did his DSc degree at the University of Edinburgh in 1980.

He is a professor of chemistry and head of the Stoddart Mechanostereochemistry Group at Northwestern University, USA. In his career, he has guided 300 PhD and postdoctoral researchers.

235. Jacques Dubochet (1942-)

Jacques Dubochet is a Swiss scientist born in 1942 at Aigle. He won 2017 Nobel Prize in Chemistry for the developemnt of cryo-electron microscopy for the determination of structure of biomolecules in solution. 

He studied at University of Geneva and University of Basel. He worked at the European Molecular Biology Laboratory of Germany.

Currently, he is an honorary professor at the University of Lausanne, Switzerland.

236. Robert H Grubbs (1942-2021)

Robert Howard Grubbs was an American chemist born in 1942 at Marshall County. He received the Nobel Prize in Chemistry in 2005 for the invention of olefin metathesis.

He studied BSc and MSc at the University of Florida. He worked for doctoral degree at the Columbia University under the guidance of Ronald Breslow. He was a researcher at the Stanford University. He joined the Michigan State University as a faculty in 1969, where he started work on olefin metathesis. He was a Humboldt fellow at the Max Planck Institute for Coal Research, Germany. He moved to the California Institute of Technology as a professor in 1978.

He was a member of the National Academy of Engineering. He was a co-founder of a company to produce catalysts.

He died in 2021 at the age of 79.

237. Johann Deisenhofer (1943-)

Johann Deisenhofer is a German scientist born in 1943 at Zusamaltheim. He won 1988 Nobel Prize in Chemistry for the determination of structure of an integral membrane protein which is required for photosynthesis.

He worked for doctoral degree at the Technical University of Munich. He worked at the Howard Hughes Medical Institute and University of Texas Southwestern Medical Center at Dallas as a faculty.

He found the 3-dimentional structure of a protien present in some photosynthetic bacteria. This protein is a photosynthetic reaction center, which plays an important role during photosynthesis. He established the structure of this protein by making use of X-ray crystallography. Currently, he is working as a advisor of Scientists and Engineers for America.

238. Mario Molina (1943-2020)

Mario José Molina Henríquez was a Mexican chemist born in 1943 at Mexico City to Roberto Molina Pasquel and Leonor Henríquez. He was a recipient of the Nobel Prize in Chemistry in 1995 for the discovery of depletion of ozone layer at antarctic region by chlorofluorocarbon gases. He was the first Mexican to won the Nobel Prize in Chemistry.

He received Bachelor's degree from the National Autonomous University of Mexico in 1965. He studied polymerization kinetics at the Albert Ludwig University of Freiburg, Germany. He was graduated from the the University of California, Berkeley.

Later, he worked at the University of California, Irvin, Massachusetts Institute of Technology, California Institute of Technology, University of California, San Diego and the Center for Atmospheric Sciences at the Scripps Institution of Oceanography. He served as climate policy advisor to the President of Mexico. He received more than 30 honorary degrees.

239. Richard Errett Smalley (1943 – 2005)

Richard Errett Smalley was an American chemist born in 1943 at Akron, Ohio to Frank Dudley Smalley, Jr., and Esther Virginia Rhoads. He received the Nobel Prize in Chemistry for the discovery of buckminsterfullerene – a new form of carbon. He was also a specialist in nanotecchnology.

He studied BSc and PhD at the University of Michigan and the Princeton University respectively. He was a postdoctoral fellow at the University of Chicago.

He was a professor at the Rice University.

He died in 2005 at the age of 62.

240. Robert J Lefkowitz (1943-)

Robert Joseph Lefkowitz is an American scientist born in 1943 at The Bronx. He won 2012 Nobel Prize in Chemistry for the discovery of function of G protein-coupled receptors.

He was graduated from the Bronx High School of Science. He received BA in chemistry from Columbia College. He studied at the Columbia University College of Physicians and Surgeons for MD degree. After an internship and residence at the College of Physicians and Surgeons, he joined National Institutes of Health as clinical and research associate. Later, he was appointed as a faculty at the Duke University Medical Center. He became professor in 1977 at Duke University.

He is working with the Howard Hughes Medical Institute since 1976.

241. Louis E Brus (1943-)

Louis Edward Brus is an American chemist born in 1943 at Cleveland. He has won 2023 Nobel Prize in Chemistry for the discovery of quantum dots.

He was graduated from the Rice University in 1965. He received PhD from the Columbia University under the guidance of Richard Bersohn. Later, he worked at the United States Naval Research Laboratory as scientific staff officer at Washington, D. C. He moved to AT&T Bell Laboratories, where he discovered quantum dots. He moved to Columbia University in 1996 as a faculty. He was a fellow of the American Academy of Arts and Sciences, member of the United States National Academy of Sciences and Norwegian Academy of Science and Letters. He has received many awards and honors.

Currerntly, he is a Samuel Latham Mitchell Professor of Chemistry at Columbia University.

242. Jean-Pierre Sauvage (1944-)

Jean-Pierre Sauvage is a French chemist born in 1944 at Paris. He received the Nobel Prize in Chemistry in 2016 for his ground-breaking research on supramolecular chemistry.

In 1967, he was graduated from the National School of Chemistry of Strasbourg. He received PhD degree from the Université Louis-Pasteur under the guidance of Jean-Marie Lehn, who was a 1987 Nobel laureate. During his doctoral degree study he worked on the first synthesis of cryptand ligands. He was a postdoctoral fellow under the supervision of Malcolm L. H. Green.

In addition, he has also worked on electrochemical reduction of carbon dioxide, molecular topology, catenanes, molecular knots and mechanically-interlocked molecular architectures. He was a member of the French Academy of Sciences.

Currently, he is working at the Strasbourg University as emeritus professor.

243. Kary Banks Mullis (1944 – 2019)

Kary Banks Mullis was an American scientist born in 1944 at Lenoir to Cecil Banks Mullis and Bernice Barker Mullis. He got recognition for the invention of polymerase chain reaction technique. He received the Nobel Prize in Chemistry in 1993 for this work.

He received BSc from the Georgia Institute of Technology in 1966. In 1973, he received PhD degree from the University of California, Berkeley by working on bacterial siderophore. He was a postdoctoral fellow at the University of Kansas Medical Center and the University of California, San Francisco. Later, he worked for Cetus Corporation, molecular biology for Xytronyx. He was a distinguished researcher at the Children's Hospital Oakland Research Institute.

244. Richard Royce Schrock (1945-)

Richard Royce Schrock is an American chemist born in 1945 at Berne, Indiana. He won the Nobel Prize in Chemistry for his work on olefin metathesis.

He studied BA at the University of California, Riverside and PhD at the Harvard University. He was a postdoctoral fellow at the University of Cambridge. He worked for DuPont. Later, he moved to Massachusetts Institute of Technology (MIT) as a faculty and became a professor in 1980.

He is a member of National Academy of Sciences and American Academy of Arts and Sciences. He has received many awards, prizes and honors.

Currently, he is an emeritus professor at MIT and distinguished professor at the University of California, Riverside.

245. Richard Henderson (1945-)

Richard Henderson is a British scientist born in 1945 at Edinburgh. He is a pioneer in the area of electron microscopy of biomolecules. He is a recipient of 2017 Nobel Prize in Chemistry for the invention of cryo-electron microscopes.

He was graduated from the University of Edinburgh, postgraduated from Christi College, Cambridge and received PhD from the University of Cambridge. He worked on structure and mechanism of chymotrypsin for his PhD degree under the guidance of David Mervyn Blow at the MRC Laboratory of Molecular Biology. He was a postdoctoral researcher at Yale University, where he worked on voltage-gated sodium channels. He returned to MRC Laboratory of Molecular Biology and worked with Nigel Unwin on structure of the bacteriorhodopsin by electron microscopy.

He has been honored with many prizes and medals. Currently, he is a mentor for the Academy of Medical Sciences.

246. Alexey Ekimov (1945-)

Alexey Ekimov is a Russian chemist born in 1945. Basically, he is a solid state physicist and a pioneer in nanoscience. He is a recipient of 2023 Nobel Prize in Chemistry for the discovery of quantum dots.

He studied his graduate degree at the Leningrad State University and PhD at the Ioffe Institute of the Russian Academy of Sciences. Later, he joined Vavilov State Optical Institute, where he worked on semiconductor-activated glasses and discovered quantum dots in 1981. He postulated theories of quantum confinement with Alexander Efros.

He has received the 1975 USSR State Prize in Science and Engineering and R. W. Wood Prize. Currently, he is working in a company based in New York on nanocrystals technology.

247. Ahmed H Zewail (1946 – 2016)

Ahmed Hassan Zewail was an Egyptian and American chemist born in 1946 at Damanhur. He is considered as the father of femtochemistry. He was a recipient of Nobel Prize in Chemistry in 1999 and thus he became the first Egyptian and Arab to win a Nobel Prize in Science.

He studied BSc and MSc degrees at the Alexandria University. He moved to University of Pennsylvania to pursue PhD degree under the guidance of Robin M. Hochstrasser. He was a postdoctoral fellow at the University of California, Berkeley in Charles B. Harris's lab. Later, he joined California Institute of Technology as a faculty in 1976. He was the Linus Pauling Chair Professor of Chemistry at the California Institute of Technology.

He was nominated to participate in President Barack Obama's Presidential Council of Advisors on Science and Technology.

248. Paul Lawrence Modrich (1946-)

Paul Lawrence Modrich is an American scientist born in 1946 at Raton, New Mexico to Laurence Modrich and Margaret McTurk. He received 2015 Nobel Prize in Chemistry for his work on DNA mismatch repair.

He studied at the Massachusetts Institute of Technology for BS Degree and at the Stanford University for PhD degree. He was a postdoctoral fellow at the Harvard Medical School in Charles C. Richardson's laboratory.

Later, he joined the University of California, Berkeley as assistant professor in 1974. He moved to Duke University in 1976. He has received Pfizer Award in Enzyme Chemistry, Charles S. Mott Prize, Robert J. and Claire Pasarow Foundation Medical Research Award, Feodor Lynen Medal, etc. He is a fellow of the American Academy of Arts and Sciences and member of the National Academy of Sciences and National Academy of Medicine.

He is a James B. Duke Professor at Duke University and he is also working for Howard Hughes Medical Institute since 1995.

249. Aziz Sancar (1946-)

Aziz Sancar is a Turkish scientist born in 1946 at Savur. He is a molecular biologist specialized in cell cycle checkpoints, DNA repair and circadian clock. He received 2015 Nobel Prize in Chemistry for the study of DNA repair. He has studied photolyase and nucleotide excision repair in bacteria.

He received MD degree from Istanbul University in 1969 and PhD from The University of Texas at Dallas in 1977 under the guidance of Claud Stan Rupert.

Currently, he is a professor of biochemistry and biophysics at the University of North Carolina School of Medicine. Besides, he is the co-founder of the Aziz & Gwen Sancar Foundation, which promote the study of Turkish students in USA.

250. Roger David Kornberg (1947-)

Roger David Kornberg is an American scientist born in 1947 at St. Louis. He won 2006 Nobel Prize in Chemistry for his work on determination of the way in which information from DNA is copied to RNA.

He received BSc degree from the Harvard University in 1967 and PhD degree from the Stanford University in 1972. He was a postdoctoral fellow at the Laboratory of Molecular Biology in Cambridge, UK. Later, he joined the Harvard Medical School as an assistant professor in 1976.

Currently, he is a professor of structural biology at Stanford Medical School since 1978. He is also the editor of the Annual Review of Biochemistry since 2004.

251. Thomas Robert Cech (1947-)

Thomas Robert Cech is an American chemist born in 1947 at Chicago. He is a recipient of Nobel Prize in Chemistry in 1989 for the discovery of catalytic behaviours of RNA. He was able to find that RNA might cut itself strands of RNA. He postulated that life might have started as RNA. Besides, he was able to find that RNA can speed up biological reactions in addition to transmiting

instructions. He discovered an enzyme telomerase reverse transcriptase, which is a part in the process of restoring telomeres when thay are shortened during cell division.

He received his doctoral degree from the University of California, Berkeley. He was a postdoctoral fellow at the Massachusetts Institute of Technology. Later, he joined the University of Colorado as a faculty. Currently, he is a distinguished professor there. He promoted science education when he was the president of Howard Hughes Medical Institute.

Currently, he is teaching at the University of Colorado.

252. Aaron Ciechanover (1947-)

Aaron Ciechanover is an Israeli scientist born in 1947 at Haifa. He is the recipient of the 2004 Nobel Prize in Chemistry for the determination of way in which cells degrade and recycle proteins using ubiquitin.

In 1974, he was graduated from Hadassah Medical School in Jerusalem. He worked for PhD degree in Technion – Israel Institute of Technology in Haifa. He was a postdoctoral fellow at the Massachusetts Institute of Technology.

He was a visiting fellow at the National Cheng Kung University, Taiwan. He has opened the Ciechanover Institute of Precision and Regenerative Medicine at Shenzhen. Ha has received many awards and prizes.

Currently, he is a distinguished professor at the Ruth and Bruce Rappaport Faculty of Medicine and Research Institute at the Technion.

253. Martin Lee Chalfie (1947-)

Martin Lee Chalfie is an American scientist born in 1947 at Chicago. He has won 2008 Nobel Prize in Chemistry for the discovery of green fluorescent protein. He was married to Tulle Hazelrigg.

He studied for PhD degree at the Harvard University. He was a postdoctoral fellow at the Laboratory of Molecular Biology.

Later, he became a faculty at the Columbia University in the department of biological sciences.

He was a member of the National Academy of Sciences. He has published around 100 research articles. He has won Golden Goose Award in 2012 in addition to the Nobel Prize. He received an honorary degree from the University of Parma.

Currently, he is a professor at the Columbia University.

254. Michael Levitt (1947-)

Michael Levitt is a South African-born scientist born in 1947 at Pretoria. He is a recipient of Nobel Prize in Chemistry in 2013 for the development of multiscale models for complex chemical systems.

He studied at the University of Pretoria and King's College London. He was a PhD student at the Peterhouse, Cambridge. He did part of his research at the Weizmann Institute of Science, Israel. Later, he moved to the Stanford University as a teacher. He was a research fellow at Gonville and Caius College, Cambridge as well. He is one of the pioneers to conduct research on simulation of molecular dynamics of DNA and proteins. As a consequence, he developed a software for this purpose.

He was a founding co-editor of the journal 'Annual Review of Biomedical Data Science'. Currently, he is working as a professor of structural biology at the Stanford University since 1987.

255. Akira Yoshino (1948-)

Akira Yoshino is a Japanese chemist born in 1948 at Suita. He received the Nobel Prize in Chemistry in 2019 for the creation of safe production-viable lithium-ion batteries.

He studied BSc and MSc degrees at the Kyoto University and doctoral degree at the Osaka University. He spent all his life at Asahi Kasei Corporation, which is a non-academic career.

He initially worked on polyacetylene and later he turned his interest towards the development of rechargeable batteries. He has won many prizes including Chemical Society of Japan, Battery Division Technology Award, Ichimura Prizes in Industry, Yamazaki-Teiichi Prize, Global Energy Prize, Charles Stark Draper Prize.

Currently, he is a professor at the Meijo University since 2017 and a honorary fellow of the Asahi Kasei Corporation.

256. Hartmut Michel (1948-)

Hartmut Michel is a German scientist born in 1948 at Ludwigsburg. He has won the Nobel Prize in Chemistry in 1988 for the determination of structure of an integral membrane protein (which is essential to photosynthesis) by X-ray crystallography.

He studied at the University of Tübingen in Dieter Oesterhelt's laboratory. He received the Gottfried Wilhelm Leibniz Prize and the Bijvoet Medal. He is a member of German Academy of Sciences Leopoldina, Royal Netherlands Academy of Arts and Sciences and the Royal Society.

Currently, he is the director of the Department of Molecular Membrane Biology at the Max Planck Institute for Biophysics. Besides, he is also working as a professor of biochemistry at the Goethe University, Frankfurt.

257. Peter Agre (1949-)

Peter Agre is an American scientist born in 1949 at Northfield. He received the Nobel Prize in Chemistry in 2003 for the discovery of channels in cell membranes. He discovered aquaporin protein channels, which move water molecules through cell membrane.

He studied BA at the Augsburg University, MD at Johns Hopkins School of Medicine. He was trained at Case Western Reserve University and North Carolina Memorial Hospital as well. He returned to Johns Hopkins School of Medicine to join Vann Bennett's lab. He was a faculty at the Department of Medicine. He served as the Vice Chancellor of the Duke University Medical Center.

Currently, he is a distinguished professor at the Johns Hopkins School of Medicine and the Johns Hopkins Bloomberg School of Public Health. He is also a director of the Johns Hopkins Malaria Research Institute. He is the President of the American Association for the Advancement of Science.

258. Bernard L Feringa (1951-)

Bernard Lucas Feringa is a Dutch chemist born in 1951 at Barger-Compascuum to Geert Feringa. He married Lies Feringa née Hake. He is a recipient of the Nobel Prize in Chemistry in 2016 for the design and synthesis of molecular machines. Basically, he is specialized in homogeneous catalysis and molecular nanotechnology.

He studied MSc and PhD at the University of Groningen. Later, he joined the same university as lecturer in 1984 and promoted as professor in 1988. In the beginning he worked on oxidation catalysis, homogenous catalysis, enantioselective catalysis, asymmetric hydrogenation, photochemistry and stereochemistry. He has developed light driven molecular rotary motor and a molecular car driven by electrical impulses. He has patented 30 research works, published more than 650 articles and guided over 100 PhD students in his career. Currently, he is a Jacobus van 't Hoff distinguished professor at the University of Groningen and an academy professor of the Royal Netherlands Academy of Arts and Sciences. He is living in Paterswolde near Groningen.

259. Gregory Paul Winter (1951-)

Sir Gregory Paul Winter is a British scientist born in 1951 at Leicester. He received the Nobel Prize in Chemistry in 2018 for his work on the therapeutic uses of monoclonal antibodies. He worked at the MRC Laboratory of Molecular Biology and the MRC Centre for Protein Engineering based at Cambridge in his entire career.

He was graduated from the Trinity College in 1973. He received doctoral degree from the MRC Laboratory of Molecular Biology under the supervision of Brian S Hartley. He was a postdoctoral fellow at the Imperial College London and the University of Cambridge.

He is the fellow of the Trinity College.

260. Venkatraman Ramakrishnan (1952-)

Venkatraman Ramakrishnan is a Indian-born British-American scientist born in 1952 at Chidambaram to Prof. C. V. Ramakrishnan and Prof. Rajalakshmi. He won the Nobel Prize in Chemistry in 2009 for his work on structure and function of ribosomes.

He studied BSc at the Maharaja Sayajirao University of Baroda and obtained PhD degree from the Ohio University in 1976. He also worked at the University of California, San Diego where he trnasformed his interest from physics to biology. He was a postdoctoral fellow at the Yale University, where he worked on ribosomes. He continued this research as a scientist at Brookhaven National Laboratory from 1983-1995. Later, he joined the University of Utah in 1995 as a professor of biochemistry. In 1999, he moved to Cambridge's Laboratory of Molecular Biology.

He worked at the Medical Research Council's Laboratory of Molecular Biology at Cambridge. He is a fellow of the Trinity College and served as the president of the Royal Society between 2015 and 2020.

261. William Esco Moerner (1953-)

William Esco Moerneris an American chemist born in 1953 at Pleasanton to Bertha Frances and William Alfred Moerner. He is a recipient of the 2014 Nobel Prize in Chemistry for his work on spectroscopy of a single molecule in condensed phases.

He studied his undergraduate degree at the Washington University in St. Louis and graduate degree at the Cornell University. Later, he worked at the IBM Almaden Research Center located at California. He was a visiting professor at ETH Zurich and the Harvard University. He joined the University of California, San Diego in 1995. In 1998, he moved to the Stanford University. Currently, he is working on biophysics.

262. Morten Peter Meldal (1954-)

Morten Peter Meldal is a Danish chemist born in 1954. He received 2022 Nobel Prize in Chemistry for his work on development of click reactions.

He received BS and PhD degrees from the Technical University of Denmark. He was a postdoctoral fellow in the same university and then at the Cambridge University and the University of Copenhagen. Later, he joined the Technical University of Denmark as assistant professor.

Currently, he is a professor at the University of Copenhagen.

263. Brian Kent Kobilka (1955-)

Brian Kent Kobilka is an American scientist born in 1955 at Little Falls. He received the Nobel Prize in Chemistry in 2012 for his work on discovery of functions of G protein-coupled receptors.

He studied BSc degree at the University of Minnesota Duluth and MD at the Yale University School of Medicine. He was also trained at Washington University in St. Louis and Barnes-Jewish Hospital. He was a postdoctoral fellow at the Duke University under Robert Lefkowitz. Later, he joined the Stanford University in 1989 and moved to Howard Hughes Medical Institute in 1987.

His research group determined the molecular structure of the β2-adrenergic receptor, which has been cited more number of times by other scientists.

He also received John J Abel award for his notable contributions in the area of pharmacology and Javits Neuroscience Investigator Award.

He was a member of the National Academy of Sciences. Currently, he is a professor at the Stanford University School of Medicine's department of Molecular and Cellular Physiology.

264. Roderick MacKinnon (1956-)

Roderick MacKinnon is an American scientist born in 1956 at Burlington. He received 2003 Nobel Prize in Chemistry for his work on the structure and function of ion channels. He was married to Alice Lee.

He was educated at the University of Massachusetts Boston and Brandeis University. Later, he entered Tufts University for MD and joined Beth Israel Hospital for training in internal medicine. He was not satisfied with the medical profession, hence he joined Christopher Miller's laboratory at Brandeis University as a postdoctoral fellow. He moved to the Harvard University as an assistant professor in 1989, where he worked on X-ray crystallography and methods of protein purification. He joined Rockefeller University in 1996 as a professor, where he worked on the structure of the potassium channel, which exists in cell membrane. Currently, he is working as a professor at Rockefeller University.

265. Frances Hamilton Arnold (1956-)

Frances Hamilton Arnold is an American chemist born in 1956 at Edgewood. She has won the 2018 Nobel Prize in Chemistry for her work on directed evolution to engineer enzymes.

She was educated with BS degree from the Princeton University. Later, she worked as an engineer in Brazil, South Korea and Solar Energy Research Institute at Colorado. She joined the University of California, Berkeley to pursue PhD degree. She moved to the California Institute of Technology as a visiting associate.

Currently, she is a Linus Pauling professor at the California Institute of Technology. She is serving as an external co-chair of the United States President Joe Biden's Council of Advisors on Science and Technology.

266. Koichi Tanaka (1959-)

Koichi Tanaka is a Japanese scientist born in 1959 at Toyama. He won 2002 Nobel Prize in Chemistry for the development of new methods for mass spectrometric analyses of bio-macromolecules. 

He studied at the Tohoku University for bachelor's degree. Later, he joined Shimadzu Corporation, where he worked on development of mass spectrometers. For the analysis of bio-macromolecules like protein by mass spectrometry, it has to be ionized and vaporized by LASER. During this process, the molecules may break. To overcome this limitation, Tanaka has developed a new matrix for ionization.

267. Robert Eric Betzig (1960-)

Robert Eric Betzig is an American scientist born in 1960 at Ann Arbor. He received the Nobel Prize in Chemistry in 2014 for his work on development of super-resolved fluorescence microscopy. 

He studied at the California Institute of Technology for BS degree. Afterwards, he joined Cornell University. He received MS and PhD degree in 1985 and 1988 respectively. For doctoral degree he worked on developement of high-resolution optical microscopes.

Later, he joined AT&T Bell Laboratories, where he was able to image fluorescent molecules at room temperature. For this work, he was awarded the William O. Baker Award for Initiatives in Research and William L McMillan Award. Afterwards, he moved to Ann Arbor Machine Company. He returned to academia by joining Okemos, Michigan. In 2006, he joined Janelia, where he developed super high-resolution fluorescence microscopes. In 2016, he became an academician of the Pontifical Academy of Sciences. Currently, he is working as a professor at the University of California, Berkeley.

268. Moungi Bawendi (1961-)

Moungi Bawendi is an French-born American chemist born in 1961 at Paris. He won 2023 Nobel Prize in Chemistry for his work on quantum dots. He was married to Rachel Zimmerman.

He studied at the Harvard University for AB and AM degrees. He received PhD from the University of Chicago in 1988 under the guidance of Karl Freed and Takeshi Oka. He was a postdoctoral researcher at the Bell Labs. Later, he joined the Massachusetts Institute of Technology in 1990.

He received many awards like Nobel Signature Award, Sackler Prize and Ernest Orlando Lawrence Award. He was a member of the American Association for the Advancement of Science, American Academy of Arts and Sciences and National Academy of Sciences.

Currently, he is working as a Lester Wolfe professor at the Massachusetts Institute of Technology.

269. Paul Anastas (1962-)

Paul Anastas is an American chemist born in 1962 at Quincy. He is considered as the father of Green Chemistry. He has designed 12 principles of green chemistry.

He studied at the University of Massachusetts Boston for BS degree and at the Brandeis University for MA and PhD degrees.

He served as the scientific advisor to the United States Environmental Protection Agency. Besides, he was an assistant administrator to the Research and Development appointed by Former President of USA Barack Obama.

Currently, he is working as the Director of the Center for Green Chemistry and Green Engineering at Yale University.

270. Stefan Walter Hell (1962-)

Stefan Walter Hell is a Romanian-born German scientist born in 1962 at Arad. He is the recipient of 2014 Nobel Prize in Chemistry for the development of super-resolved fluorescence microscopy.

He studied at the Heidelberg University for his doctoral degree under the guidance of Siegfried Hunklinger on imaging of transparent microstructures in a confocal microscope. He worked at the European Molecular Biology Laboratory situated in Heidelberg. He joined University of Turku as a group leader. He was a visiting scientist at the University of Oxford. He was a director of the Max Planck Institute for Biophysical Chemistry.

Currently, he is working as one of the directors of of the Max Planck Institute for Multidisciplinary Sciences and Max Planck Institute for Medical Research, which are based in Germany. Besides, he is the leader of the German Cancer Research Center's Optical Nanoscopy division. He is an honorary professor at the University of Göttingen since 2004.

271. Jennifer Anne Doudna (1964-)

Jennifer Anne Doudna is an American scientist born in 1964 at Washington, D.C. She is a recipient of the Nobel Prize in Chemistry in 2020 for the development of a method for genome editing.

She was graduated from Pomona College and pursued PhD from Harvard Medical School.

Currently, she is a professor at the University of California, Berkeley's department of molecular and cell biology. Since 1997, she is also working at the Howard Hughes Medical Institute.

She is a founder of the Innovative Genomics Institute. She is a faculty at Lawrence Berkeley National Laboratory and an adjunct professor at the University of California, San Francisco.

272. Carolyn R Bertozzi (1966-)

Carolyn Ruth Bertozzi is an American chemist born in 1966 at Boston. She received the Nobel Prize in Chemistry in 2022 for her work on click chemistry and bioorthogonal chemistry.

She received BA degree from Harvard University and later joined Bell Labs. In 1993, she received PhD degree from the University of California, Berkeley under the guidance of Mark Bednarski. She was a postdoctoral fellow at the University of California, San Francisco. Afterwards, she joined UC Berkeley College of Chemistry as a faculty and as scientist at Lawrence Berkeley National Laboratory.

She is a member of the National Academy of Sciences, the National Academy of Inventors etc. She received many awards such as MacArthur "genius" award, Lemelson–MIT Prize etc.

Currently, she is a professor at the Stanford University. She is also associated with the Howard Hughes Medical Institute.

273. Emmanuelle Charpentier (1968-)

Emmanuelle Marie Charpentier is a French scientist born in 1968 at Juvisy-sur-Orge. She is specialized in biochemistry, genetics and microbiology. She is a recipient of 2020 Nobel Prize in Chemistry for the development methods for genome editing.

She studied at the Pierre and Marie Curie University and Institut Pasteur. She was a postdoctoral fellow at the Rockefeller University. She was an assistant research scientist at the New York University Medical Center and research associate at the St. Jude Children's Research Hospital. Later, she started her independent career at the University of Vienna.

She is the director of Max Planck Institute for Infection Biology based at Berlin. She has established the Max Planck Unit for the Science of Pathogens.

274. Benjamin List (1968-)

Benjamin List is a German chemist born in 1968 at Frankfurt. He has won the Nobel Prize in Chemistry in 2021 for his work on asymmetric catalysis. He married Sabine List in 1999.

He studied MSc at the Free University of Berlin and PhD at the Goethe University Frankfurt. He was a postdoctoral fellow at the Scripps Research Institute, USA. He was a group leader at the Max Planck Institute for Coal Research and became its director later. He is considered as the pioneer in organocatalysis. He has explored the applications of proline as a chiral catalyst. He is a recipient of many honors and awards.

Currently, he is one of the directors of the Max Planck Institute for Coal Research, honorary professor at the University of Cologne since 2004 and he is also working at Hokkaido University since 2018. He is the editor of the chemistry journal Synlett.

275. David W C MacMillan (1968-)

Sir David William Cross MacMillan is a Scottish chemist born in 1968 at Bellshill. He received the Nobel Prize in Chemistry in 2021 for his work on asymmetric organocatalysis.

He studied his undergraduate degree at the University of Glasgow under the supervision of Ernie Colvin and PhD degree at the University of California, Irvine under the guidance of Larry Overman. For his doctoral degree he worked on the development of stereocontrolled bicyclic tetrahydrofurans. He also worked on the total synthesis of 7-(−)-deacetoxyalcyonin acetate – a diterpenoid isolated from *Eunicella stricta*. He was postdoctoral fellow at the Harvard University. Later, he started his independent career at the University of California, Berkeley and later moved to Caltech. He was the founding editor of the journal Chemical Science. Currently, he is a distinguished professor at the Princeton University.

9 7 9 8 8 9 4 4 6 5 5 8 6